To read *Evading Death's C*
Long's detailed account of his ret
memorable to me. There is so mu~~ch~~ ~~to be learned from Steve's book~~,
especially by those who question the existence of spiritual warfare
and God's omnipotence.
 Glenn Chrisman
 Magazine Editor

Enjoyed this book immensely from a number of standpoints.
Steve's renditions of the NDE's, especially his personal one, very
provocative and challenging. His command and presentation of
the Christian doctrines plus scriptural documentation extremely
instructive, humble, and persuasive...excellent primer for any of
us...New Jerusalem, heaven, spiritual warfare discussions, helpful
appendices, and the Q and A sections likewise, very helpful to anyone,
new or old in theology. In short, this book really turned me on!
 William H. Targgart, MD

Dr. Steven Long has taken a series of near death experiences,
starting with his own as an unusual means to present the Gospel
and its importance to everyone. I don't believe that anyone could
read this book without being challenged to consider the life changing
importance of the Biblical Gospel, that "Christ died for our sins
according to the scriptures" as the key to an abundant, eternal life.
While not many will have the kind of near death experiences that Dr.
Steven describes for both himself and others, no one can doubt the
veracity of what he has to say and his own conclusions. Knowing
Steve personally through many discussions at a men's Bible study, I
appreciate his thorough knowledge of the scriptures, their authority
and their application to every one's life experiences which he brings
out so well in this book.
 John H. Jenks
 Retired civil engineer

The urgency of choosing wisely for eternity has never been
presented more forcefully than in Dr. Steven Long's new book,
Evading Death's Grip. Beginning with a riveting account of a 2014
heart attack and subsequent NDE's that changed and refocused his
entire life, Steve goes on to present in the starkest terms possible
the consequences of choosing for God – and choosing against Him.
Steve's message couldn't be clearer – don't wait until you're in your
own white room to get your eternal destiny settled. Do it today. Highly
recommended.
 Edward Schmeichel
 Professor (emeritus), San Jose University

1

Steve Long returned from 20 plus years in Taiwan to head the International Students Christian Outreach program at Stanford. It was being sponsored by our church in nearby Menlo Park. He joined the men's fellowship group at the church where we became friends. Even prior to his near death experience, Steve had a fascinating life. In the 20 plus years he and his wife Vicky lived in Taiwan, they created a program for the schools called Global Champions. This program, taught in middle school, enhanced the lives of more than three million children there. They now are working to bring this program to U.S. schools. Steve's experiences escaping death is an awe-inspiring story that awakens new vistas in your thinking. I think you will enjoy this book very much.

Paul Ely
Retired Management Executive, Hewlett Packard

If you've ever wondered what happens after death as we know it, you've got to hear about it from someone who's experienced it! Steve's genuine narrative implores the reader to give important thought the implications of our present choices on our eternal future, and challenges everyone to choose the path to light over darkness.

Audrey K. Bowden, PhD
Assistant Professor, E.E., Stanford University

Dr. Steven Long's book *Evading Death's Grip* is one the most important books that a believer or non-believer can read. The author had his own Near Death Experience (NDE) which he details for the readers. And he did extensive research on other people NDEs. He reasonably concludes that destiny (eternal life) "is not a matter of chance; it's a matter of choice." Ours!

Duane E. Clapp Jr.
Retired lawyer, Menlo Park, California

If you have even a passing interest in eternal life, Near Death Experiences (NDEs), and good and evil, you should read *Evading Death's Grip*, by Dr. Steven W. Long. Dr. Long vividly writes about his journey of faith—from skeptic to follower of Christ—and how his experience with an NDE and other's experiences helped form a biblically consistent framework to consider for eternal life and the battle between good and evil in the world. Faith is a decision. Reading *Evading Death's Grip* may be just what you need to make that decision.

Skip Vaccarello
Business leader, author of "Finding God in Silicon Valley'"

This book will provoke you to consider a sobering reality... "everyone on earth will live forever"! It's a revelation we must explore before it's too late, and Steve's firsthand experience, along with countless others he has researched, should draw you to believe there is much more to our existence than a good career, relationships, and even charity. I believe God imparted these visions to Steve for the purpose of changing many more lives than his own, and this book is part of it fulfilling it. Steve's life is a witness to what is written inside these pages. Praise God for all that He will do through this book!

Grace Yanni Han
Stanford University Master's Student

Gracefully interweaving Scripture while interspersing his own personal account as well as the experiences of others, Steve poses poignant questions which lead the reader to reflect on their own experience of God ... Love unites our tripartite nature: our spirit, our soul, and our body. Steve's near loss of his bodily self provides him a unique vantage point from which he considers the forever-living aspects of our being: own spirit and our soul. Ultimately, the book is not as much a depiction of Steve's near death experience as it is a meditation on living a Christ-centered life. Gone, but not gone, Steve describes his near death *experience as a regeneration; born again into a new beginning from above.*

Professor Doug Leigh
Pepperdine University, California

EVADING DEATH'S GRIP

College Professor Experiences
Supernatural Life After Death

DR. STEVEN W. LONG

EVADING DEATH'S GRIP
Dr. Steven W. Long

Copyright © 2017 by Dr. Steven W. Long

ISBN: 978-0-942507-90-4

Unless otherwise noted, all scriptures are from the NEW AMERICAN STANDARD BIBLE ®, Copyright© 1960, 1962, 1963, 1968, 1971, 1972, 1973, 1975, 1977, 1995 by The Lockman Foundation. Used by permission.

Scripture quotations marked (NKJV) are taken from the NEW KING JAMES VERSION®. Copyright © 1982 by Thomas Nelson, Inc. Used by permission. All rights reserved.

Scripture quotations marked (NIV) are taken from THE HOLY BIBLE, NEW INTERNATIONAL VERSION®. Copyright © 1973, 1978, 1984, 2011 by Biblica, Inc.™. Used by permission of Zondervan

Bracketed statements inserted in scriptures are commentaries or explanations by the author.

Address all personal correspondence to:
Dr. Steven W. Long
P.O. Box 15745, Stanford, CA 94309, USA
website: www.evadingdeathsgrip.com
email: evadingdeathsgrip@gmail.com

Individuals and groups may order books from Dr. Steven W. Long directly, or from the publisher. Bookstores and other retailers should refer to the Deeper Revelation Books website for distribution information, as well as an online catalog of all our books.

Published by:
Deeper Revelation Books
Revealing "the deep things of God" (1 Cor. 2:10)
P.O. Box 4260
Cleveland, TN 37320 Phone: 423-478-2843
Website: www.deeperrevelationbooks.org
Email: info@deeperrevelationbooks.org

Deeper Revelation Books assists Christian authors in publishing and distributing their books. Final responsibility for design, content, permissions, editorial accuracy, and doctrinal views, either expressed or implied, belongs to the author.

CONTENTS

DEDICATION

This book is dedicated to all those who are seeking to know if God is real, to those in need of healing, and to those involved in helping others receive healing, both medically and spiritually. May this book encourage and inspire you to press forward with more passion to see the captives set free from the bondages of sin, sickness, and death, through the supernatural power of God, His word, and His people.

ACKNOWLEDGMENTS

We want to acknowledge all those who participated in Dr. Steve's fight for life because of an out-of-hospital massive heart attack while in Taiwan. We are eternally grateful to all those who helped Steve survive a life-threatening traumatic crisis. There were so many involved in this intervention.

Thanks to the medical teams: paramedic team, Intensive Care Unit, doctors, surgeons, nurses, hospital administration and staff, hospital interns, and volunteers.

Thanks to those who prayed for Steve. Most of all, thanks to God who spared and extended his life.

We know that the love and power of God brought Steve through. It takes teamwork to bring healing to those in crisis. Only around 12% survive out-of-hospital cardiac arrests in the United States. Steve is more than a survivor. He is a miracle!

Victoria Lynn Long

Therefore, being always of good courage, and knowing that while we are at home in the body we are absent from the Lord ... we are of good courage, I say, and prefer rather to be absent from the body and to be at home with the Lord (2 Corinthians 5:6-8).

On Death's Edge

Some physical actions, feelings, and cognitive thoughts can help us—others can hinder or even keep us from the best paths for our lives. One of my choice ways of communicating this truth is the following statement that I have made many times through the years: "How we react intellectually and emotionally is our choice."

In this introduction, I think you need to know me and some of my history. I was born and raised in the Midwest in the United States to a loving family and raised in a business environment in a very small town.

My mom took my brother and me to Sunday School and church from the time she could carry us. Dad was the founder/manager of a truck stop, motel, and restaurant. He also serviced the farms in the area with diesel, propane, and gasoline. Consequently, he did not attend church often, especially when his business went to twenty-four hours a day and seven days a week. Though I was born into and brought up in a Christian church, I did not believe—so as soon as possible I quit attending.

When I was a teen, it seemed the biggest thing to do on a Saturday night was to go to a movie. The county I lived in was "dry" (meaning no alcohol) so a person would have to drive to the next county around twenty miles away to buy any. I mention this because as soon as I was old enough to purchase alcohol I would have some occasionally. Though I did not admit it then, upon reflection, I think I was slowly becoming an alcoholic by the age of twenty.

I joined the United States Air Force during the Vietnam era, which did not help my addictive tendencies. At the end of the four-year experience in the Air Force, I allowed my hair to grow long and had a beard as well. I ran with a crowd who were hippies, and even though we were seeking truth, we were not actually seeking God. I went through several life-shattering events that influenced me to come to faith in God. I was involved in a youth movement called The Jesus People. It consisted mainly of those of us who had come from the counter culture of the hippie movement. You can imagine us: long hair and beards, wild and colorful clothing, and having spiritual awakenings of all types.

While I was growing and learning about the spiritual life, I met and married my wife, Victoria (Vicky). She has been a wonderful partner and one of the most stable factors in my life. We started out our married life with her teaching school while I was working in the aircraft industry.

That soon ended when we pursued a life in ministry and serving others. We were trained in Switzerland and traveled extensively throughout Europe, the Middle East, and Israel. Then we pastored a church in Southern California for several years. Even during this time, my thoughts would occasionally reflect upon the addictions I had developed in my youth, though I did not actually yield to these temptations and go back to the habits of the past.

Flash forward many years, I've admitted to others and myself, "I have always had an addictive nature." I am not able to do things in a small way. Almost everything I have done in life, I've done "to the max." These statements are a true self-assessment. From my "growing up" years till a few years ago, no matter what I have done, I always seemed to "overdo" it.

This lifestyle of addiction followed me through the Air Force and into civilian life. The weakness toward alcohol and other addictions did not just drop away, but each thing has been a raging battle to fight for lasting change in the mind and in actions as well. I recall quitting smoking in my early twenties and throwing cigarettes away by the pack for a period of over three months prior to finally gaining the victory and never returning to them.

This inner nature of weakness toward addiction was intertwined with the development of habits that strengthened the ties. Also, at a very early age, I experienced exposure to pornography as well and was hooked for many years in my teens and early adulthood. Then, after deeply committing my life to the Lord, He led me into a life of service for Him and not serving my own lustful desires.

Even when drinking coffee or other drinks, I

would allow myself to drink more and more. In the case of coffee, I would start out having a cup a day, but soon that became two, then three, and up to at least seven or eight cups of this black brew. I would brew up to two pots full of the stuff each morning at work—and this was as far back as my thirties. Though I would quit drinking it occasionally, I would always go back to it soon after. I started and stopped doing these kinds of things over and over throughout my life, only to start doing them again.

Even as I entered a profession of serving others as a pastor and missionary, the thoughts from the past would plague me occasionally. I found that trying to do other things to satisfy this addictive nature from my past (trying to overcome these inappropriate, plaguing thoughts) only tended to make it worse. As a "man of the cloth," occasionally I would cave in to the temptation, sneak a peek or have a beer, only to feel overwhelmed with self-condemnation afterward.

I Looked OK on the Outside

As a teacher, pastor, missionary, university professor, husband, and father, I seemed to have it all together on the outside. I could put on a front and act like I was OK, but on the inside, I knew I was not. I thought and acted like much more of a spiritual person than I was. This is the compromising condition I was in when I had my sudden heart attack. That one event brought everything crashing down and motivated me to fight my way through to complete personal victory.

God is not as interested in what we do for Him as He is with who we are. His chief concern is the genuineness of our friendship with Him and others. I was doing lots of things for Him: having many meetings, speaking, teaching and praying for others, and all the while, I was slowly slipping away from Him. I had a "religious routine," but my friendship with Him was diminishing. The old addictive tendencies were influencing me to run on vapor. The river of His presence was flowing through me, yet sadly, it was not always flowing to me.

Transformation Was Needed

Then, just three years ago, I was forced to slow down. It was not an option. I had to reflect on the food, drink, and behavior patterns that were unhealthy. The reason: a major heart attack, triple bypass surgery, and the subsequent out-of-body experiences and Near-Death Experiences (NDEs). The heart attack happened while on a ministry trip to Taiwan. I had been running so fast, and working almost constantly without taking any time off. Because of that, I had allowed some of the old habits to return into my thought life. I am convinced that the main reason for the heart attack was my failure to address issues and allowing them to dominate my thoughts. This could have led me to actions that would have been very harmful to me and to others. Now, I can truthfully say, that my former addictive nature has been dealt with and I am celebrating recovery from a lifetime of being controlled by these issues.

It's not an easy matter to deal with (to talk about, or to write about) these things, and these addictions did not go away with a simple prayer. To just pray and not dig deeper is like placing a Band-Aid on a cancer, thinking that the cancer will just go away. I believe God allowed me to have the heart attack, ultimately for my good. Conveniently, my doctor was reputed to be one of the best heart surgeons in Taiwan for bypass surgeries. However, it was God who brought me through the twenty-three days of hospitalization.

Now, years since the heart attack and subsequent flat lining (dying) nine times, I've received help and have learned a lot. Along with others, I am celebrating my recovery, not only from the heart problems, but also from a life of addictive behaviors. The future holds transformation from my old struggles, the outcome of being more and more like the grace filled Savior who set me free.

If there were no reasons for me to go on and nothing more God wanted to do through me, He would have simply taken me home to heaven from Taiwan, but He did not do that. Therefore, I believe He has a far greater purpose and ministry through me in the future. I am so excited to be alive so I can participate with Him in this unfolding destiny. I believe the future will be even more amazing than the past. As I consider all that He has done in the past, it is exciting to imagine and hope for the future.

For a righteous man falls seven times, and rises again (Proverbs 24:16).

Talking to God Needed!

You and I will need prayer (more than ever), as we prepare for, and embark on, the new future ahead of us. I invite you to go on a wild journey, similar to a spiritual roller coaster ride. As the hobbit, Bilbo Baggins, would say, "We are going on an adventure!"—one that continues in a far better place than earth can offer. This journey will ultimately lead us into the heavenly realms to experience the amazing realities far beyond our ability to imagine.

Many of my friends firmly believe that the enemy of our souls, Satan, put an assignment out to kill me. This may be the case with you also (possibly because he knows that the future will be exponentially brighter and more power-filled than the past). However, it was not God's will or timing for me to transfer to heaven just yet, because there is much, much more work to be done here on the earth.

This book is written as a preparatory to help us continue until the change occurs. This change will be the end of life as we know it. There will be an amazing adventure into a world, a universe, and a kingdom that is thousands of times more exciting than this one we are leaving behind.

I am humbled and very relieved that God has a plan for each of us. I am convinced that all I have been through brought me to a point of absolute surrender and dependence upon Him: His plan, His mercy, and His love.

I welcome you to join in pursuit of this awesome God who has a plan for your life as well. His blood cleanses us from all the wrong we've ever done, and His hand delivers us from evil. Our choices to follow Him completely, and get help, are the responses He is looking for.

Please seek Him with me and He will allow us to find Him (Matthew 7:7). I encourage you to become a "Follower of Jesus" like me, but without a heart attack wake-up call. Come with me on this wonderful journey.

Dr. Steven W. Long

CHAPTER ONE

Fictional Movies and Eastern Spiritual Perceptions

"Doctor, I was dead and now I'm alive." These were my words as they wheeled me to my new room six-and-a-half days after my entrance into the Intensive Care Unit. The doctors and nurses in the ICU had been able to keep my body working while I recovered from my heart attack even though my heart failed to keep beating several times. I had a new lease on life, but it did not feel much like it physically. Spiritually I was made aware of things that previously I was oblivious to (and how often that is the case).

This is the story of my adventure at the edge of death. It is also about the discussion with the doctor about what I encountered. It was worth it, because I returned with a narrative of the experience of a lifetime (or death time, to be more correct).

In the West, fictional movies, have been popular for young and old alike. Perhaps you have seen or heard of them. If you have, you've probably come to an understanding (even though it is a fictional representation) that there is a supernatural force— in reality, two forces. These exist in an unseen realm as close as our very breath, yet completely invisible to most eyes. Fantasy, like the movies portray, may be very closely related to spiritual reality while the same time, light years removed.

For those who've not seen many of these, the movies suggest that there exists a "Force" that can be manipulated for good or evil. There is also an Eastern spiritual concept of equal opposite forces in the universe. The reality is that on one hand, there exists a host of heavenly beings and a powerful kingdom of light. This kingdom has a loving, all-powerful King. The King can be influenced by our willingness to do things His way and when we participate in His plan, but I don't think we could manipulate Him.

On the other hand, there is a kingdom of darkness that can at times be felt. Its beings desire to make the kingdom of light non-effective on people living here. This dark kingdom also has a leader. It has many, many malevolent beings who are bent on our destruction, on displacing the kingdom of light and its ruler, and on defiling all that is good and pure. There is a deception among the human believers in this dark kingdom that somehow, they can manipulate this power and these beings. Possibly the reality is the humans are being manipulated while thinking that it is they who are doing the manipulation.

So, we have been thrust into this earth realm,

surrounded by both good and evil beings who, for the most part, are invisible. There are dark, malevolent powers ruled by the prince of darkness, along with a myriad of peaceful and loving beings ruled by the King of Light. The two kingdoms are locked in a longtime conflict, doing battle for sovereign dominion over each one of us.

Imagine, currently around us a war is raging that we are not able to see or hear or, for many of us, even comprehend its very existence. Only occasionally do we really sense someone just feet from us who is either from one side or the other. These waring influencers want to persuade and encourage us to follow them through our choices. I don't know if this makes sense, but I suspect many of you reading this have had these feelings; that there are others who we only "feel" around us and, though we don't quite see them, we know they are here.

Have you ever asked, "Why did this happen?" or "Why me, Lord?" or "God, didn't You remember that we are here on the earth?" "Why have You allowed this strange, invisible battle to go on?" Have you ever even thought about the profoundness of these things? As I draw from historical, ancient literature and wisdom sources, as well as recent experiences and research, I will attempt to answer these questions, and enlighten you about the ultimate intentions of both kingdoms. These malevolent forces of darkness had an assignment concerning me in Taiwan: "Make sure he doesn't leave the hospital alive!"

The Dark Kingdom's Desire:
A Body Bag

It was a blistering evening in Taiwan, the air was so full of humidity, it seemed like I was inhaling hot water. I had just experienced an exhausting two weeks of intensive speaking engagements, communicating with thousands at a stadium rally, flights to Japan, Shanghai, and back to Taiwan, more meetings, teaching at a university in East Taiwan, sleepless nights, and back-to-back meetings. Then, on the evening of May 1, 2014, I roused from deep sleep to find myself laying, securely belted down on a bed in a hospital's Intensive Care Unit.

Standing next to the bed in front of me, I saw two hateful-eyed, wicked, nasty, mean, malignant beings who strangely appeared to be human. They looked like hospital workers, but I knew instinctively they were death's emissaries. One stood next to me glowering with bloody, red eyes. He looked like a Chinese man, dressed in a blue zippered jacket with five Chinese characters written on the back, (loose translation: spirit of death). Next to him was a seven-plus-foot-tall, amazingly skinny Chinese looking woman. As I looked at her, the thought came, *A skinny, grey-faced messenger of death, dressed in black.*

Who were they? Were they real people trying to get me, hallucinations or possibly actual demonic beings sent from the kingdom of darkness with an assignment? Why were they allowed into the Intensive Care Unit and who let them in? All I knew was that they were in the hospital room and, in my perception, their intentions were evil. I thought to myself, *Their eyes look like those of demons I've seen and even cast out in the past in the name of Jesus, but, how could this be since they were also seemingly human?*

Bad news! I quickly discovered that I could not simply speak and see them leave, as I had done in the past. Various tubes protruded from my mouth and nose, and I was not able to talk. More about the deadly duo later.

I think I was convinced that there were people trying to kill me. Because of fear, I thought there was poison in the IVs. I kept pulling them out from the back of my hands, arms, and even feet, while the staff kept trying to find new places to get the life-giving liquids and medicine into my body. Could it be that a powerful outside force had come upon me and was trying to take my life in this way? I was told later that I could even get out of any type of restraint that was used to keep me from pulling IVs out or hurting myself.

Was I going to awaken just to find that it was a reaction to the food last night? Was this real or just a very bad dream?

Chapter 1: Q & A

Note: suggested answers are located in the back of the book.

1. What is the difference between the eastern understanding of "the Force" or "the Forces" (as popularized in some modern movies) and the one introduced in this book?

2. How do the two spiritual kingdoms manifest themselves on earth?

3. Have you ever even thought about the two spiritual kingdoms?

4. Do you think that there are actual spiritual beings bent on destroying us?

5. Is there a way to have victory over addictive behavior?

6. Are there ways to keep ourselves from having a heart attack, even when heart disease is hereditary or is in our DNA?

CHAPTER TWO

The Battle, Mayday! On May Day

"Call the ambulance immediately; we have a massive heart attack victim on the thirteenth floor."

The morning air was filled with the screams of sirens on May 1, 2014, as an ambulance made its way through heavy, congested Taipei traffic. Minutes later, I was sprawled on the couch having a massive heart attack. I had previously pulled myself up from the bathroom floor where I had passed out and was sweating profusely. I popped a nitroglycerin tablet into my mouth hoping to prevent my death while awaiting help. Then I opened the front door of the apartment to let the paramedics and a fellow co-worker in.

Not arriving at the train station on time to meet my interpreter and go to a university had alarmed him. Calling emergency, he sent a fellow staff member to the apartment to find me.

I have no recollection of how the paramedic team came to the thirteenth-floor apartment and wheeled me out on a gurney. I was not conscious and have no memory of the incident, only knowing what happened from hearing others talk about it. The ambulance rushed me to the nearest hospital. My heart would not keep beating, in fact, it flat-lined six times while in the ambulance, so the EMTs kept me alive by defibrillation.

At the same time, the paramedics called the hospital's top heart surgeon to meet us at the emergency room. Though he was on his way home after a busy, long day at the hospital, he returned to take care of me. We later discovered that this doctor happened to be rated the number one heart surgeon in all of Taiwan. It was amazing that this was the closest hospital when I was in critical need. The more we read, research and see, the more we understand that God is in control of everything.

Coincidence or God-incidence?

Does God in fact know everything? Upon reflection of the events leading up to this heart attack, it is obvious that nothing takes God by surprise. He doesn't say, "O, I never thought of that one." The Scriptures state, *"And we know that God causes all things to work together for good to those who love God, to those who are called according to His purpose"* (Romans 8:28).

Note: the statement is not "God causes all things," but rather that He causes all things to work together. He does not cause all things but, He does cause all things to work together for His glory and our good! We don't always understand how God is doing this but we can trust Him. Consider the following:

- I could have been flying to Japan, to Shanghai, or back to Taiwan, and yet I had the heart attack very close to a hospital.

- I could have had a doctor who had little experience, and yet the one who performed the open-heart surgery was reputed to be the very best.

- My heart could have stopped and not revived, and yet, even though it did stop a total of nine times, it eventually started beating on its own.

- I could have been a bad statistic—one of the 88%—as only approximately twelve out of a hundred people who have heart attacks outside a hospital live to tell about it, and yet I am still here.

Even though I had overdone it physically through my own wrong choices, God was there to bring me through and give my life back to me many times. There are no coincidences in God's kingdom.

A Deleted Memory

For two weeks prior to the heart attack, till two days before my hospital stay ended (forty-seven days later), to this day, the only thing I physically remember of the emergency room is when the technician asked me if I could take off my wedding ring. I said, *"I don't think so."* The paramedic said he was sorry, but he had to cut it off. I groaned and said, "Oh no!" That's all I remember, except for one other conversation that Vicky (my wife) had with me. I will tell that story later.

Come on, Heart—Beat!

As my physician was assessing the situation, my heart continued to fail to keep beating. The doctors decided that I needed triple bypass open heart surgery, so the procedure began immediately, as soon as they could get one of our Champions leaders to sign the waiver and approval to do surgery. My heart had to be shocked three times during the surgery with the result of burns on my back where the electrodes were placed. My back looked like a hot iron had been in a fight with me (and won), as they had burned me in a couple of places. The physical fight for my life was in full throttle!

My life was in the hands of God, many people's prayers, and the hands of the doctor and his team of assistants. The medical team was fighting for my life because I was not able to fight for myself, and was put on life support to keep me alive until my heart could start beating on its own.

Unaware of all that was taking place on the ground, Vicky, my wife of thirty-seven years, was in the air on the twelve-hour flight from San Francisco headed for Taiwan. She arrived at midnight, looking forward to seeing me and beginning the big twentieth anniversary celebrations of Global Champions (GC), the international education association we co-founded. After a brief greeting by our GC CEO and leadership team at the airport, they gently asked her to please not panic as they told her what had happened. After this, they rushed her to the Intensive Care Unit to see me and pray for me.

Note: GC does work in Taiwan, doing business as Champions Education Association of Taiwan. CEA was started approximately twenty-five years ago by Victoria (Vicky) and Dr. Steven Long. Its purposes are to help youth face problems, have good emotional management, gain life skills, and encouraged team leadership and participation.

Three hours after the surgery, Vicky arrived to the whir of machines that were keeping me alive. The doctors lowered the dose of the sleep medication so I could regain consciousness; to test if I recognized her voice since they thought, *I might be brain dead or damaged due to oxygen starvation for such a long time.* Vicky's voice awakened me with the words, "Hi Steve, it's Vicky, I love you and I am here now and everything is going to be OK."

I awoke and opened my eyes and recognized her. I tried to speak to her, but with all the tubes in my mouth and nose could not talk. She said I looked frightened and I attempted to speak.

The only words that kind of came out sounded like "Die" and "Help me." Vicky asked me if I had a bad dream, and I nodded my head "Yes" and tried to speak, but could not. As you will read, it was much more than just a bad dream. Actually, it was a bad reality.

I do not remember any of the physical things surrounding the situation, so I will let Vicky tell you what happened next. I remember the spiritual realities, and she remembers the physical facts.

Vicky's Chronicle

Steve was lying down in the hospital bed with tubes, wires, and IVs connecting him to many monitors and machines. The sounds of beeping and pumping noises filled the air. The Doctors were very pleased that Steve recognized me, but they immediately raised the medications to sedate him again, because he was thrashing around trying to free himself from the bed and get up and out of there. He needed to stay calm and not so agitated so he could recover from the surgery better.

According to the doctors, Steve was in very critical condition when I arrived at the hospital. The surgery was successful, but time would tell how successful his recovery would be. They could not release him from the Intensive Care Unit until he passed several tests to ensure his conditions had stabilized. Steve was in very critical condition due to the emergency nature of the surgery. Normally, he would not even had been able to have surgery if any of these conditions were present.

First, he was on blood thinners for his previous heart condition where they had inserted several stents years before; there were tubes draining blood from the incisions into a half full bucket on the floor. He was not able to quit bleeding!

Second, he had congestion in his lungs from a severe cold he caught while in China a few days before. So, tubes from his mouth and nose drained the infection from his lungs. Generally speaking, a person doesn't receive surgery when an infection is in their body.

Third, his heart was not beating on its own, it needed an external pacemaker with wires through his chest connected to it.

Fourth, he had oxygen starvation to his brain due to the amount of time he was in the apartment before the ambulance came and the number of times his heart stopped, and they had to revive him before and during the surgery. It was not apparent how much damage had occurred. They explained that he could come to and be in a vegetative state. These conditions had to stabilize before he could move from the Intensive Care Unit.

WOW! There we were, two English speaking American Caucasians, across the Pacific Ocean in Taipei, Taiwan, in a Medical Hospital with Chinese speaking doctors and nurses. What an unexpected turn of events. Our plans for a few weeks of celebrations for a twentieth Anniversary of Champions, an education association we founded, had radically changed into a critical fight for life. In one defining moment of time, everything had changed forever.

Fortunately, we were in good hands with a good medical team, and our Champions staff was working on getting hundreds of people praying for a miracle. We definitely needed a big miracle to be able to get Steve off the medical life support systems and back on his feet in good health. We had no idea that God had already anticipated our dilemma and planned to use it to perform a wondrous work in our lives.

Chapter 2: Q & A

1. Does anything catch God by surprise?

2. Does God cause all things?

3. Can you give an example how something worked out for your good and God's glory?

CHAPTER THREE

Conflicting Kingdoms, Violent Spiritual Realities

Do you remember the two beings I started telling you about earlier? Well, here's what happened.

Every time the doctors and nurses distanced themselves from me, the short, blue jacketed man would walk up next to me and throw something looking like black powder on my face. Then the woman would come near and pull a black bag over my head, tightening its draw strings and constricting the bag around my neck until my breathing stopped.

Apparently, their assignment was to rob me of life! Each time the deadly duo approached and attempted to fulfill their assignment for me, I would hear my breathing quit and then my heart would stop as I lost consciousness.

Nevertheless, a short time later I would revive and come back to life. Each attempt to end my life eventually failed. I sensed a calm unlike any I'd ever known, and almost felt like saying to them, "Go ahead, you cannot kill me!" each time they tried. I have no idea how long a time this abusive attack continued, or how many times the deadly duo approached and did it, but I was more and more exhausted as the hours, then days went by.

I was not able to physically fight them and seemed to be frozen and unable to move. I could feel the restraints on my arms and legs semi-effectively tying me down on the bed that kept me from resisting as I lay in that extremely cold room. Another reason I was restrained, as I found out later, was that I could not distinguish the doctors and nurses from these two uninvited and unwanted visitors, and occasionally, I would strike out at the staff or doctors and kick them if they approached me.

Who Were These Uninvited Guests?

They almost certainly were angelic beings who had lost their heavenly position by following Lucifer. His name meant "brightness or morning star," and in his great prideful deception long ages ago, he misled about a third of the angels. Note: the Bible alludes to the fact that one-third of an innumerable company of angels chose to rebel with Lucifer, whose name was changed to Satan.

John (in the last book of the Bible, Revelation 12:3-9) saw this great sign in heaven, an enormous red dragon [a type of Satan]. His tail swept one-third of the stars—metaphorically, angels who chose to follow him—out of the sky and flung them to the earth. The great dragon was hurled down, that ancient serpent called the devil, who leads the whole world astray. He was hurled to the earth, and his angels with him. The result was that they morphed into demonic creatures.

We must do a little spiritual history lesson to understand this more fully. Undoubtedly, my visitors were two of these fallen, demonic beings. There were countless angelic beings in heaven created by God as He unfolded the universe. The only three named angels in the Bible whom apparently held leadership roles were Michael, Gabriel, and Lucifer, whose name meant "bringing or providing light." It is believed that Satan used his musical instruments created within his being to be the worship leader of heaven. *"The workmanship of your timbrels and pipes was prepared for you on the day you were created"* (Ezekiel 28:13, NKJV).

As you will see later, he chose to try to become "the big guy" (God) because of his huge ego and pride. He convinced many of these supernatural beings to join him in rebellion against the one true God. Satan and his host lost the war in heaven and were banished to the earth!

Why Are They Here?

Questions have plagued me since those eventful hospital days: questions that need answers. And, what an adventure answering those questions is. So, come along and learn what I've found out. Why were fallen angels on earth? Why were they in that hospital room trying to destroy me? And, why were they picking on me anyway?

As time went by, it became apparent to me that these two beings had an assignment from the dark side, the kingdom controlled by an enemy, Satan. Their assignment: to make sure that I would not walk out of the hospital alive but rather be carried out in a body bag!

I don't know with certainty all the answers behind the personal attack on my life, and I don't think of myself as very important in my own eyes, but it may have to do with several things. Remember what I wrote about having an "addictive nature." It is very likely that I'd opened the door, giving them an invitation through my own actions and choices over the years.

Also, as the co-founder, along with my wife Vicky, of Champions Education Association, one of the largest youth movements in Asia, it may be that the devil just wanted to take me out—thinking that would have a devastating effect on the organization. So, he sent these two spiritual thugs, who were supposed to do the job. The dark kingdom wants to destroy anyone and anything relating to the kingdom of light.

I quickly found out that I could not stop them, and I could not get free by myself. After many times of passing out and being near-death (if not actually dead), I finally realized what I must do. You will see this too. What must I do?

The Name Above All Other Names

Back in the hospital room … I seemed to remember statements I'd heard people say over the years. Most were something like, "When in trouble, call on the name of Jesus." First, call on Jesus. I started weakly doing that; I would exhale a whisper, "Jesus" and inhale "Is my Lord" in every breath. I had so little strength that that was all the energy I could muster, but it was enough. His strength started filling me. I could literally feel something like electricity flowing into my body and filling me head to feet.

Then, second, I somehow remembered that I needed to address the attackers—after being infused with and regaining His strength, I told the little man to tell the woman that it was OK if they did not complete this assignment. Then, I stated, "In the name of Jesus, stop!" At the mention of the name of Jesus, they stopped, glared at me, turned and quickly and quietly left the room. The Bible instructs us to "resist the devil and he will flee from you" (James 4:7). So, I did and he did.

Although they left the room, I was still not free to move; I had been restrained because of the extreme agitation I experienced when they were close (though the doctors and nurses did not realize this cause). I was not sure if they were gone. They left the room but were they still in the hospital, or if they were still in the hospital somewhere, were they awaiting another occasion to continue with the attack? In either case, I seemed to be at least temporarily free from this evil onslaught.

Again, why did God see fit to send these hateful beings to the earth? Surely, this thought has plagued many people who have a variety of answers. My answer is more of a practical explanation than a theological theory or endeavor.

The Church (we who have asked God to forgive

everything we've done wrong, and have received His life within us, and declared Jesus, His Son, as Lord) is described in the Bible as God's ARMY, as overcomers, as victorious.

Statements About God's ARMY (us)— Christ's Soldiers

No soldier in active service entangles himself in the affairs of everyday life, so that he may please the one who enlisted him as a soldier (2 Timothy 2:4).

Finally, be strong in the Lord and in the strength of His might. Put on the full armor of God, so that you will be able to stand firm against the schemes of the devil. For our struggle is not against flesh and blood, but against the rulers, against the powers, against the world forces of this darkness, against the spiritual forces of wickedness in the heavenly places. Therefore, take up the full armor of God, so that you will be able to resist in the evil day, and having done everything, to stand firm (Ephesians 6:10-13).

The thought has come to me, *How can we learn to be overcomers, a victorious and conquering ARMY ... without an enemy and a war?* Could it be that God allowed these beings who are hell-bent on our destruction to be here on earth purposefully?

If God Is All Loving—Then, WHY?

So, let's see ... this God who is supposed to be loving and is in fact light and love, has cast the devil and all these demons who followed him and delight in nothing more than killing, maiming, confusing, and ruining humans through warfare-like tactics ... yes folks, God has cast them to the earth where we live—billions (possibly trillions) of them, if not more. WHY? We will discuss this as well as other questions in the next chapter.

Chapter 3: Q & A

1. Do you think there are actually personal, individual beings (demons) who are dispatched to do bad and ugly things to those of us who live here on planet earth?

2. How much power is available in the name of JESUS? (See Matthew 28:18 below.)

3. Is Jesus' power (authority) somehow transferable? (Please see John 14:12, Mark 16:15-18 below.)

And Jesus came up and spoke to them, saying, "All authority has been given to Me in heaven and on earth" (Matthew 28:18).

Jesus said, "Truly, truly, I say to you, he who believes in Me, the works that I do, he will do also; and greater works than these he will do; because I go to the Father" (John 14:12).

And He said to them, "Go into all the world and preach the Gospel to all creation. He who has believed and has been baptized shall be saved; but he who has disbelieved shall be condemned. These signs will accompany those who have believed: in My name, they will cast out demons, they will speak with new tongues; they will pick up serpents, and if they drink any deadly poison, it will not hurt them; they will lay hands on the sick, and they will recover" (Mark 16:15-18).

CHAPTER FOUR

Benevolent Dictator, Malevolent Foe

The fact that the kingdom of darkness, Satan, and demons are real hardly needs to be stated as we look around and try to gain an understanding of the conditions on planet earth today. As we read the Bible and other texts and take a quick perusal of history, the reality of evil's existence is all too evident.

As real as God, His kingdom, His truths, and angels, so an opposing kingdom is declared loudly to those who are willing to listen. Yet, the fact that the opposing kingdom is here by no means suggests that it is equally as powerful. Also, the distortion of and misrepresentation of either and/or both kingdoms through their respective subjects is acknowledged over the centuries and millennia since men and women have been on earth.

The Big Bang Theory

Regardless of your beliefs (even atheists have a belief system empowered by their faith in science), there was a time when everything we can see and perceive of the universe was not here. Some call what happened the "Big Bang," while other belief systems allow faith in a creative being who is personal, and wants to have relationship with humankind, and intelligently designed everything; and still others have many, many different and distinctive belief systems.

It is not my intention to discuss the validity of any of these theories, but to move on with a pre-supposition: a Judeo-Christian worldview, which is my personal background, and is supported by the Near-Death Experiences (NDEs) I've had and researched over the last few years. It is, then, from a Biblical perspective of believing in God that I will describe why some beings who share the earth with us are not benevolent (well-meaning and kind), but are rather malevolent (showing a desire to do evil to others).

Though I've not thoroughly researched every religion in existence, I have learned much from my faith as a follower of God, that has grown for my entire life, except for the short departure I described earlier. As a born-again, Spirit-filled, follower of God, I have read, researched, and attempted to live by the principles of the Bible for the last forty-two years. This background affords me some credibility.

I present the following which may or may not be what you've been taught. Regardless of your understanding (or lack thereof) of the Bible, I encourage you to read this entire book and the experiences I and others have had and studied, as well as the biblical passages presented, to at least understand the underlying belief system of a Jesus follower.

War in the Heavenlies

Imagine that there are other beings who are not like us and are invisible to us, generally. They also have supernatural powers. Satan, who was called Lucifer prior to his expulsion from heaven, was one of the top three angelic beings in God's kingdom and under His authority. The true story of Satan's fall is described in two key Old Testament chapters and one New Testament passage. They are Ezekiel 28, Isaiah 14:12-16, and Revelation 12:7-9.

The first ten verses of Ezekiel 28 seem to be dealing with a literal human leader, the king of Tyre (Tyrus—KJV), but verses 11-19 provide a description so otherworldly that it couldn't possibly apply to a mere mortal man:

> *The word of the Lord came again to me, saying, "Son of man, say to the leader of Tyre, Thus says the Lord God, because your heart is lifted up and you have said, 'I am a god ... yet you are a man and not God ... With your wisdom and understanding you have acquired riches for yourself and have acquired gold and silver ... your heart is lifted up because of your riches—therefore ... I will bring strangers upon you, the most ruthless of the nations. And they will draw their swords against the beauty of your wisdom and defile your splendor. They will bring you down to the pit, and you will die ... Will you still say, "I am a god?" ... You will die the death of the uncircumcised by the hand of strangers,*

for I have spoken!' declares the Lord God!" (Ezekiel 28:1-10).

Again, the word of the Lord came to me saying, "Son of man, take up a lamentation over the king of Tyre and say to him, 'Thus says the Lord God, You had the seal of perfection, full of wisdom and perfect in beauty. You were in Eden, the garden of God; every precious stone was your covering: the ruby, the topaz and the diamond; the beryl, the onyx and the jasper; the lapis lazuli, the turquoise and the emerald; and the gold, the workmanship of your settings and sockets, was in you. On the day that you were created they were prepared. **You were the anointed cherub who covers,** *and I placed you there. You were on the holy mountain of God ... You were blameless in your ways from the day you were created* **until unrighteousness was found in you** *... therefore, I have cast you as profane from the mountain of God ... Your heart was lifted up because of your beauty;* **you corrupted your wisdom** *by reason of your splendor ... All who know you among the peoples are appalled at you; you have become terrified and you will cease to be forever'"* (Ezekiel 28:11-19).

Seemingly, the last few verses refer to the fall of Lucifer/Satan. The first ten verses are about the human leader of Tyre (who was condemned for claiming to be a god though he was just a man). The "King of Tyre," starting in verse 11, seems to have been fallen Lucifer (Satan), for there were several attributes written that could not have been those of a man. For example, this king is portrayed as having a different nature from mankind:

- He was an anointed cherub (angel)—verse 14.

- He had a different position from man (he was blameless and sinless)—verse 15.

- He was in a very different realm or place than mankind (he was found in Eden, near the throne, and on the holy mountain of God)—verses 13-14.

- He was judged differently than mankind (thrown out of heaven and onto the earth)—verse 16.

These descriptions of him were not human, but superhuman (full of wisdom, perfect in beauty, and had the seal of perfection—verse 12). Fictitiously, there must have been a mirror in heaven and when Lucifer walked by and his eye was caught by the image reflected of him, he thought something like this, *You're a handsome hunk of Angel, you are perfect and you are so good! In fact, you should be the ruler of all!* He wasn't content to lead the worship of God; instead, he coveted to be God himself.

The text informs us that this king was created in the presence of God in a perfect state (Ezekiel 28:12, 15). And he was perfect in his ways until iniquity was found in him (verse 15). His sin is related in verse 17, *"Your heart became **proud** because your beauty, and you corrupted your wisdom because of your splendor."* Lucifer apparently became so impressed with himself, his beauty, intelligence, and power, that he thought of himself as being equal with the honor and glory that were God's alone.

> *"How you have fallen from heaven, O star of the morning, son of the dawn! You have been cut down to the earth, you who have weakened the nations! But you said in your heart, 'I will ascend to heaven; I will raise my throne above the stars of God, and I will sit on the mount of assembly in the recesses of the north. I will ascend above the heights of the clouds; I will make myself like the Most High'"* (Isaiah 14:12-14).

Satan Thrown Down to Earth

Lucifer, who had a name change to Satan after his fall, somehow persuaded a great multitude of angels to join him in this rebellion.

> *And there was war in heaven, Michael and his angels waging war with the dragon. The dragon and his angels waged war, and they were not strong enough, and there was no longer a place found for them in heaven. And the great dragon was thrown down, the serpent of old who is called the devil and Satan, who deceives the whole world; he was thrown down to the earth,*

and his angels were thrown down with him (Revelation. 12:7-9).

Satan and his hoard can never win; he is self-deceived and/or possibly mentally challenged from his fall, but is quite intelligent and has a diabolical plan. He invites us to join him in hell, the place that was created for him, and his myriads of eternally ruined beings (Matthew 25:41). (Trust me, you don't want to be there; others have seen and I've heard what it is like—this place will be described later).

Why, God?

What could be the purpose of an all-knowing, all-loving God in sending millions, if not trillions, of beings to this planet who are hell-bent on destroying His kingdom and His followers? Did He forget that He created us and put us here on this earth? Is He indeed a being with the main characteristic of love?

These are questions that came to my mind when I first read the Bible over forty years ago, and saw passages indicating this scenario. Knowing God and His character, I realized He only does things out of love—even though, this seemingly was not a loving act.

Why would a loving God punish people for eternity for a limited number of wrong personal sins? That's what makes no sense to people, but I don't believe that's what is happening. When we think that we are transient beings being punished eternally for finite offenses, we are wrong. We are, in fact, eternal beings like the angels. But unlike the angels, we are being given many, many finite, temporal chances and choices on earth to choose life instead of death eternally.

> *"I call heaven and earth to witness against you today, that I have set before you life and death, the blessing and the curse. So, choose life in order that you may live, you and your descendants, by loving the Lord your God, by obeying His voice, and by holding fast to Him; for this is your life and the length of your days, that you may live in the land which the Lord swore to your fathers, to Abraham, Isaac, and Jacob, to give them"* (Deuteronomy 30:19-20).

No War—No Victory

There can be no victory without an actual war. To say that we are the victorious ARMY of a kingdom without a war to win is an oxymoronic statement. Surely there had to be a war and even though Lucifer was created perfect, he developed an imperfection. Pride was found in him and the arrogance it spawned in him got him kicked out of his position, rank, and place in heaven.

Somehow, as stated earlier, it has been assumed or implied (in Revelation 12) that he managed to convince one-third of the angels in heaven to join his rebellion, and even though conflict rages on, he won't succeed against the other two angelic beings (Gabriel and Michael the archangel) and possibly two-thirds of the angels who remained loyal.

God, in His love for us (you and me), allowed what seems to be a mistake or a very bad joke. He sent Satan and these demons (fallen angels who joined Satan) to the earth. As was stated before, I was quite shocked and upset by this fact when I first learned of it, but then I realized that unless there is war, there is no chance for victory.

Love—Not "Hooked on a Feeling"

Remember the songs, "You've Lost That Loving Feeling," by the Righteous Brothers and "Hooked on a Feeling," sung by B. J. Thomas? Regretfully, many people don't realize that feelings come and go, but choices are also an important part of love. If there is no choice of allegiance, there are merely human puppets or robots serving God and His kingdom. The only way to have allegiance is to provide a legitimate option. Love is not a feeling as much as a choice; and for us, HIS followers, to show our love, we must choose to come into and continue in HIS ways, His kingdom. One does not get there because of one's parent's faith and choice—God has no grandchildren. So, we must come away from the kingdom of darkness (which we are all born into via its permeation of planet earth through Satan's hoard of followers) and come into His light and have a loving relationship (friendship) with God the way He dictated. Yes, I used the word dictated purposefully, for God is a dictator (howbeit, a benevolent, loving one).

We've now looked briefly at the two kingdoms and their invisible influence on mankind. We have pondered questions concerning the why's and how's of a creation that is flawed from choices made long ago. And now, it begs us to understand who these kingdoms are wrangling over.

In the next chapter, we will look at who we are. In fact, without an understanding of our very nature, we can't see a connection between our death and anything eternal. But, with some understanding, we will see what happens at the point of physical death and beyond.

Chapter 4: Q & A

1. Can you point out examples of two physical or spiritual kingdoms that are diametrically opposed to each other that are on earth today?

2. If not, why do you think otherwise?

3. Do you believe that these kingdoms have equal power—i.e., Yin Yang (Asian concept)?

4. Eastern religions use concepts of equal opposite forces, or in new age, etc., the "Force" that can be manipulated for either good or evil. Why are these concepts incorrect?

5. According to the Bible, what is the origin of demons?

6. What was the cause of Lucifer's expulsion from heaven?

7. What possibly could be in the loving purpose of God to cast Satan and one-third of the angels (the deceived, rebellious ones) to the earth?

8. What kinds of love can you name? Is love just a feeling? Is it just the hormonal calling from one to another?

Who We Are

The following short study on "who we are" is important to provide information of what happens at the point of death, and seconds prior to it, as well as the transition that occurs shortly afterward. We need to study this to understand how it can be possible for someone to separate from their body, go someplace else, and then return—as, you will read later, has been the adventure of the author and numerous others that are documented. It is also important to understand that this departure from the body is not a hallucination due to a chemical change that has gone on in the brain at the point of death.

We Are Tripartite

The tripartite view of man (trichotomy) holds that man is a composite of three distinct components: body, soul, and spirit. It contrasts with the bipartite view (dichotomy), where soul and spirit are taken as different terms for the same entity.[1] The Bible informs that we are tripartite beings because we are made in the image of God. There is only ONE true God (Deuteronomy 6:4) who expresses Himself in three distinct personalities (Father, Son, and Holy

Spirit—1 John 5:7). Likewise, we also have three parts that make up our being.

When God created Adam, He said, **"Let Us make man in Our image,** *according to Our likeness; and let them rule over the fish of the sea and over the birds of the sky and over the cattle and over all the earth, and over every creeping thing that creeps on the earth"* (Genesis 1:26).

This is a reference to what theologians have called the Godhead or the Trinity, referring to the plurality of a singular being. Agreeing with this concept, The Apostles' Creed states:

"I believe in God, the Father Almighty, Creator of heaven and earth, and in Jesus Christ, His only Son, our Lord, who was conceived by the Holy Spirit, born of the Virgin Mary, suffered under Pontius Pilate, was crucified, died and was buried; He descended into hell; on the third day, He rose again from the dead; He ascended into heaven, and is seated at the right hand of God the Father Almighty; from there He will come to judge the living and the dead. I believe in the Holy Spirit, the holy catholic (universal) church, the communion of saints, the resurrection of the body, and life everlasting."

Many years ago, a believer in China related to me a story. Watchman Nee, a famous Chinese minister, was asked the question, "How do you describe the tripartite nature of God?" He responded by picking up a Bible and after showing the end of it, he stated, "This is my Bible." Turning it so the length would be seen, he stated, "This is my Bible." And then showing the front, he again stated, "This is my Bible." One book, three views.

Interestingly, Plato of ancient Greek antiquity was also convinced of man's tripartite nature. He understood the human condition to be consisting of a tripartite being (though his view was limited to considerations of the mind's trichotomy as influencing the soul, spirit, and body).[2]

Humans are also created as tripartite beings. We have three parts like the One who created us. We read in the Apostle Paul's writings that we are tripartite beings: *"Now may the God of peace Himself sanctify you entirely; and may your spirit and soul and body be preserved complete, without blame at the coming of our Lord Jesus Christ"* (1 Thessalonians 5:23).

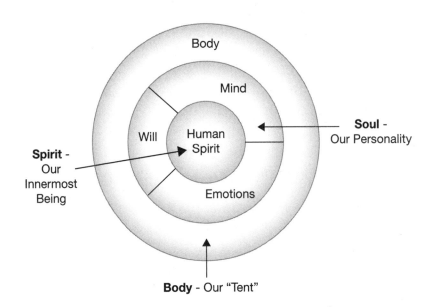

Men and women are composed of a spirit, the innermost being, a soul which consists of the mind, the will, and emotions, and a body which is like the earthly tent in which we live. When the body quits, where do we go? Some have been mentally indoctrinated to believe that when we die, there is nothing afterwards, we simply cease to exist. However, through research, this has been proven to be a misinformed opinion.

Well then, you may ask, when the tent shuts down, where do you and I go? Perhaps you have also experienced being in the hospital room with somebody, when you look at their eyes and it looks like the lights are on, but there's nobody home. I well remember a woman that we prayed for in the hospital years ago; in the first few times we were there, we could tell that she was still inside of her body by looking at her eyes. But then one time when we went back to the hospital, we realized that the body looked the same, but there was an emptiness behind those eyes. Her life (soul and spirit) had gone on somewhere else. Let me make a few statements and observations at this point.

The Body—
the House We Live in While on Earth

What do we know about people who have departed (i.e., left their bodies)? Remember, it has been presented that we are a tripartite being. When our death occurs, it is not complete death in the sense of our entire being. Rather, it is only when the tent, or physical body quits or shuts down (i.e., the heart quits beating or brain function ceases). The other two parts of us, our soul and our spirit, that are part of our personal image of God—keep going on forever.

The Soul Is Also Tripartite

Our soul is eternal—it will go on forever. Our soul (personality aspects) will depart our body when we die and our body ceases functioning. Our soul has the three following components:

1. Our mind (the ability to think and reason).

2. Our will (the ability to make choices).

3. Our emotions (the ability to have and communicate feelings).

These three components of our soul are eternal parts of our being.

The Spirit— the Innermost Part of Our Being

The spirit is essentially the life inside our entire being, the deepest part of who we are. It also will live forever joined with our soul. After God formed Adam's body out of the dust of the ground, He breathed into his nostrils the breath of life and Adam became a "living soul" (Genesis 2:7). In other words, the spiritual part of his being was awakened. God warned Adam that if he partook of the forbidden fruit he would "die" (Genesis 3:3). When Adam disobeyed, he died spiritually and began dying physically. Paul explained, *"And you He made alive, who were dead in trespasses and sins"* (Ephesians 2:1, NKJV). You see, it is when we are born again by faith in Christ that our spirit in made alive. Many people function in their body and soul but never tap into the spirit realm. It's like having a three-story house and only using two floors. The spirit is another dimension that often lies dormant in many people's lives. God's Spirit quickens or gives life to our spirit, *"But there is a spirit in man, and the breath of the Almighty gives him understanding"* (Job 32:8, NKJV).

- We are a forever living (eternal) spirit.

- We have a forever living (eternal) soul.

- We live in a mortal body (temporarily).

As stated before, in 1 Thessalonians 5:23, the most explicit example from Scripture, these divisions are written by the Apostle Paul. Also, Solomon declared, *"Watch over your heart with all diligence, for from it flow the springs of life"* (Proverbs 4:23). We see the "heart" is central to our emotions and will. It is used interchangeably with the spirit/soul amalgamation. Here is a key verse that describes the separation between soul and spirit:

*For the word of God is living and active and sharper than any two-edged sword, and piercing as far as the division of **soul** and **spirit**, of both joints and marrow, and able to* *judge the thoughts and intentions of the heart* (Hebrews 4:12).

We see in this passage of Scripture that the soul and spirit can be divided—by the Word of God (the Bible) that pierces our heart to bring the division of soul and spirit, something that only God can do. Thus, God can help us understand ourselves as we know the principles, precepts, and words of the Bible. As human beings, we live eternally as a spirit, we have a soul, and we dwell in a body. We can rejoice with the Psalmist and declare,

For You formed my inward parts; You wove me in my mother's womb. I will give thanks to You, for I am fearfully and wonderfully made; wonderful are Your works, and my soul knows it very well (Psalms 139:13-14).

Chapter 5: Q & A

1. Why talk about God being tripartite?

2. What are the three parts of human beings?

3. What happens to the body at the point of death?

4. What happens to the soul and spirit at death?

5. Where do the spirit and soul go after the body dies?

You probably stalled at question #5 thinking, *We have not discussed that in this chapter.* You're right! We are going to cover this most important subject in the next chapter. Stay tuned. In the next chapter, I am going to share with you what happened when I was "out of the body" and how that effected tremendous changes in my understanding and behavior.

CHAPTER SIX

Two Paths, Two Destinations

I've only a few vivid memories of what happened in the emergency room and in the Intensive Care Unit those fateful days in Taiwan. One of the doctors asked me if I remembered anything from the ICU (Intensive Care Unit) and when I stated "no" he emphatically replied, "GOOD!" Later, I learned why he was glad I didn't recall. Because of the spiritual attacks I was undergoing, I would sometimes get confused over who was who and would lash out at the doctors, nurses, and others who were close by.

The ICU had a group of doctors, nurses, and machines keeping my body alive. Yes, my body was basically kept going by machines for six days while I was in the Intensive Care Unit. I think all the prayers that were going on nationwide and worldwide undoubtedly had much to do with my recovery as well.

I promised earlier in this writing that I would share one of the few things I remember about the hospital experience physically. Here it is. I remember my wife, Vicky, stating that if I touched the IV that was in my carotid artery in my neck, I would die. I thought she was threatening me, but she was just stating a fact. The doctors and nurses had run out of places to put the IVs. I would get free from restraints and "rip" out the IVs—thinking that there were people trying to kill me—when truly, the nurses and doctors were trying to help me have the life-giving fluids and medications.

One more thing I've remembered; I was "floating" over my body watching a nurse who was standing next to the bed slapping my left arm. Though I could hear her, and see her from above, I had no sensation of pain. When I was in the regular room a few days later, I had a huge bruise on the left arm. I don't understand why she did this—perhaps it was to keep my mind thinking about pain while the defibrillator recharged. But the outstanding thing about it is that I remember being over my body watching. This indicates that my non-body being (spirit and soul) was released from my physical body and able to float above and observe.

Transported to Another Dimension

After the episode with the nurse happened, some of the most unusual experiences I've ever had started occurring. I had many "out-of-body" experiences along with extraordinary visions of the spiritual realm while in the ICU six-and-a-half days plus the twenty days in 24/7 nursing room.

More Real Than the Material World

Some of them, I will attempt to describe to you. Note: from my research as well as experience I found that the new body we will have when we leave our earthly body is amazing—its abilities are way beyond this normal, physical one.

There Are Angels

In recent years, there have been many books written and a lot of talk about angels. Some of the books undoubtedly are well researched and documented, however, I find a few things we need to say about the angels I've seen and the ones who are documented in the Bible. They are supernatural beings and have powers differing from ours (even in our new bodies). They do not look human (though they may be able to do so—Hebrews 13:2). Almost all who appeared in the Biblical text had to tell the humans to whom they appeared, *"Do not fear."* They had a rather fearful appearance or intimidating presence.

There Are Different Positions of Authority Among Angels

I could sense and see angels in the room with me. They were just as real as you and I are. These angelic (and fallen angelic) beings, who were there with me in the ICU and 24/7 rooms, were really there. I was just given the ability to see them. Others could feel them occasionally, but not see them.

One very interesting characteristic about the fallen angels or demons was that they seemed to be in human form (though not very convincing) while the good angels I was seeing (even with my physical eyes) were in their natural angelic form.

Note: I was not out of the body to observe these

supernatural beings—I could see them with my physical eyes. How awesome they are and what beautiful beings. It would be wonderful to see them all the time.

There Are Demons

As already described, I could literally see the two beings that had the assignment of taking me out (killing me)! I was not supposed to leave the hospital alive. I will not describe them in any more detail than I already have. Suffice it to say that all of us are in process of learning about the spiritual realities that surround us in the invisible realm. There are definitely at least two realms; the natural one we live in, and the supernatural one we don't see; however, we live in them both at the same time.

Seeing God's Very Presence

The intensified presence of God can often be felt and occasionally people can see this unusual manifestation. God is light (1 John 1:5), God is love (1 John 4:8), God is a Spirit (John 4:24), and God is … there many, many other descriptors—I will attempt to communicate some of what I've seen and experienced and continue to experience to this day.

Out-of-Body Experiences, NDEs and Other Experiences

During the time in the hospital and up to the writing of this book, I've had some wonderful supernatural gifts, one of which is I can see the presence of and the intensity of Holy Spirit's anointing almost all the time. Let me explain.

God Is Light

You may ask, "What does that look like?" I will de-scribe the experience as best I can. I continued seeing these phenomena when I was in the hospital room. When people came to visit, some of them would be surrounded by an intense light presence that they were unaware of. Others would come into the room and there would be only a small amount or none of these unusual phenomena. It was and is still perceivable to my natural eyes. I was not seeing something from inside of me, for there was a difference in the amount on various individuals. Have you ever seen a lightning bug or as we used to call them fireflies (the scientific term is Lampyridae)? These are small beetles that fly in the evening and light up their tail to attract mates, etc.

In my hospital room, occasionally I would have someone visit—one pastor that I specifically recall came and from the time he entered the doorway, I had to shade my eyes. It was like several million fireflies were swarming throughout the entire room, zooming around at an amazing speed, and blinking energetically. When he left most of them left with him and we were back to the normal in the room.

Another time, a university ministry leader came into the room, but this time it was different, I could see all the "speedy light particles" flying around my arm and hand. When I shook hands, they transferred to him and his wife. I don't think they could see what

I was seeing, but they both started weeping and I was given words to speak to them to encourage and comfort them in the work of the Lord.

There is a biblical parallel to the experience of seeing into the supernatural realm, though in the biblical case the person did not see millions of flying, wildly blinking light particles. The description of what happened is from 2 Kings 6 in the Old Testament. Elijah, who was a prophet who walked with God and had many miracles happen through and around him. His servant, Gehazi, had the following experience with God opening eyes to see beyond the natural.

> *Now when the attendant [Gehazi] of the man of God had risen early and gone out, behold, an army with horses and chariots was circling the city. And his servant said to him, "Alas, my master! What shall we do?" So, he answered, "Do not fear, for those who are with us are more than those who are with them." Then Elisha prayed and said, "O Lord, I pray, open his eyes that he may see." And the Lord opened the servant's eyes and he saw; and behold, the mountain was full of horses and chariots of fire all around Elisha* (2 Kings 6:15-18).

In a similar way that God opened the eyes of Gehazi, He also opened my eyes to see into the spiritual realm. In fact, I had the experience of seeing His light particles several years prior to my heart attack. While seated in an airplane flying from

East Taiwan to Taipei, I noticed something outside the window like a million lightning bugs were flying next to the airplane.

As I looked, these small, quick moving specks of light came right through the window and rested all over me. Then, as fast as they had appeared, they departed and disappeared. I pondered this experience the rest of the flight. I did not fully understand but I knew that something supernatural had happened.

Why? You may ask, "Why do these strange light manifestations of God's presence happen?" I will illustrate with an example.

Shortly after I was released from the hospital in Taipei, we were sitting in a restaurant and the waitress came to take our order. As I started to give my order, I noticed a huge amount of these God-light particles all over her. I prayed and ask God what this meant. No answer. Then, after the meal, she came back and I asked her if I could share with her about the unusual experiences I had in the hospital. We talked a few minutes, and I asked her, leading into a Gospel sharing, "Have you ever done anything wrong?" She reflected for a minute, and then said, "NO."

Usually, when I encountered this abruptness, the conversation ended, but this time I seemed to be led to share the "white room" experience (I'll explain later). As she listened, I could see the increase of the light particles and I asked if she would like to get to know God and she said, "Yes." We prayed and she started tearing as she took the card of the church worker who was with us.

I've seen this phenomenon over the last few years and it does not seem to be leaving. I think it is to increase my faith that God is about to do something, along with other reasons. Another example of a visible manifestation of God happened when Jesus was baptized in the Jordan River. The anointing came upon Jesus as the Holy Spirit descended in the form of a dove.

> *And the Holy Spirit descended upon Him in bodily form like a dove, and a voice came out of heaven, "You are My Beloved Son, in You I am well-pleased"* (Luke 3:22).

Though this instance did not involve countless particles of light zooming around, nonetheless, it is an instance of humans being given supernatural vision into the spiritual realm.

> *This is the message we have heard from Him and announce to you, that God is Light, and in Him there is no darkness at all* (1 John 1:5).

The difference between the dark side and His light is quite easy to discern; I will attempt to describe them as we follow along the path of some of the visions and experiential things that have happened.

A White Room Like No Other

Imagine yourself being out of your physical body, still alive, but with a different body, and then imagine yourself in a white room. No lights are on but you still see light without windows or doors. And you are trying to figure out where you are—read on to see what else you would experience!

Sometime in the first week nearing the end of my stay in the ICU, I found myself out of my body again and standing in a white room. As I looked around, though there were no lights, or switches to turn on light, the room glowed with a light. Also, there were no doors or windows to this unique room. I thought to myself, *There is no way in or out of here.* I looked around and walked close to the middle of the room that was approximately fifteen feet square, attracted with what looked like an eighteen-inch brushed aluminum disc laying on the floor. As I looked at the disc, I realized that I could see into it. It was a hologram of some kind and in it was a miniature earth hanging in space and turning. It was an exact replica. (Or was I looking at it through a portal?)

Delusion, Delirium, or Reality?

I can unequivocally state that my experiences were not just a vision somehow conjured up inside my mind. I was there! I know the difference, because I have experienced hallucinations before. For instance, one of the inhalers which I had to use to keep my lungs free from pneumonia and other infections would cause amazing visions. At one time, I told a visitor that I was seeing three-inch bumble bees walking on my bathroom door and I knew that they were merely drug-induced visions.

These out-of-body experiences that I've had,

as well as those of people I've studied (later in the next chapter), are not hallucinations brought about by medications, brain chemistry changes, or lack of oxygen. Interestingly, in his book *Imagine Heaven*, John Burke documents many people's NDEs and their encounters like a white room, or in a tunnel ending either in light or pitch blackness and various other types of experiences people who came back from death's door had. In his research, he found that no drug administered could duplicate the NDEs or "out-of-body" experiences.[3]

One such NDE was that of a young woman born blind. Her name was Vicki. Here are a few excerpts from her NDE—*"I've never seen anything, no light, no shadows, no nothing,"* she told Dr. Kenneth Ring, a professor at the University of Connecticut. He was a skeptic at the very least. Even in her dreams, Vicki didn't see anything—she just used her other senses in them. She was in an accident and thrown from the vehicle with many life-threatening injuries.

The next thing she recalled is that she was above the accident "looking" down on it. Apparently, she had left her body; for she found herself hovering just below the ceiling at the medical center. She watched a male doctor and a woman working on a woman's body—she thought, *What am I doing up here? I thought, this must be me, I'm dead?*[4]

Even someone "born blind" who doesn't know the difference between colors, when out of the body, can see. This experience authenticates the experiences of thousands and thousands of others, who haven't said anything for fear. I encourage you to contact us if you've had similar experiences. We want to document them and continue to prove that they are real. Contact us at this book's email: evadingdeathsgrip@gmail.com.

Vicki's experience was real, as was the white room that I experienced. It was, in fact, a place. I was outside my own earthly body and had a new body as I looked at the disc. I won't go into detail about the body I had, except to encourage others to read Burke's book. My body had the same characteristics as he describes in Vicki's experience.

The Uniqueness of My Personal Experience

As I was silently standing there gazing into this amazing hologram, an extraordinary thing happened. Two paths seemingly shot from the earth. One went up and out to end in darkness that was so pitch black it could be felt. The other path went to an amazingly brilliant light. The light was not earthly, for though it was very bright, it did not hurt my eyes.

Being curious, I put my foot on the path leading to darkness. I will relate that experience in the next chapter. I quickly withdrew my foot and placed the other one on the path that ended in light. At the end of the path to light, I observed that the brilliance of the light contained a far greater spectrum of light than we have on earth.

I cannot explain the colors, but it was beautiful,

and standing way, way off in the distance, at the end of the path, was a silhouette of a person. I knew intuitively that it must be Jesus; his beard and his eyes (of fire) were the same that I'd read about in the Bible. In my vision, I could zoom in on Him and then zoom back.

As I was adjusting to the extreme brightness of the light, it seemed that a huge tidal wave of LOVE came over me. I was being overwhelmed by light and love and knew that it was God who was doing that to me. The thought came to me, *I now understand why those who have gone from their bodies and experienced this light and love from the heavenly realm don't want to come back.*

The uniqueness of my out-of-body experience in the white room was that I was given a glimpse into both ends of the paths that our lives can follow. We either choose one or the other. Many other's experiences were of them already being on a path that ended up either in what they describe as nothingness, or darkness or light, or incredible beauty.

Everyone Born on Earth

Finally, I pulled my foot from that path and was still standing in the white room. Then, I heard a voice speaking to me these words. "Everyone born on earth will live forever!" As a follower of God for over four decades, I knew these words to be true, but it was as if they burned into my being, sinking into my heart.

Something changed inside me that has been permanently altered! Everyone I look at, speak to or write to (including you) will live forever and because I know that and I also know the reality of the white room, the paths, the darkness, and the light/love, it gives me a tremendous sense of responsibility.

Can We Put Off the God Decision Until We Die?

As I was talking to a physical therapist the question was raised, "So, is it OK to wait till we get to the point of death to make the God decision?" I stated, "I believe I was given the vision/experience of the two paths to provide a greater understanding. We need to decide what path we will walk on before we enter death and separation from the body. If we have heard, then we need to respond." For those who have heard, the writer of Hebrews in the Bible says, *"It is appointed once for man to die, and after that, judgment"* (Hebrews 9:27).

You may ask, "What about those who have never heard?" I don't know for sure, but God, based on His character, would not allow the ignorant to go into eternal darkness without some sort of a remedy. We know that God will deal fairly with those who have not received a direct presentation of the Gospel, just as He will deal fairly with those who have. But is God's way too narrow? Far from it. God's way is wide enough for everyone willing to accept it and receive Christ.

The most important question any of us can

answer is the one Jesus asked His own disciples, *"But what about you? Who do you say I am?"* (Matthew 16:15, Mark 8:29, Luke 9:20).

But, for those of us who have heard the Gospel (you and me), we must make this choice quickly, even today, even now. Please don't wait. Heaven is real and the "outer darkness" also is real. This earthly life is merely a vapor—it will be over very quickly.

I've had several conversations with those who have had similar experiences. At the University, I was sharing my NDE with a couple of people with the barber listening. He interrupted and asked, "Were you in the white room?" I said "Yes" and "Why, were you?" To which he said, "Yes, I died on the operating table as the doctor was doing heart surgery in 1999 and was instantly out of my body and in a white room." That is further confirmation that the afterlife is real.

Chapter 6: Q & A

1. Have you heard other people's stories about their spirit floating out of their bodies?

2. What did you think?

3. Have you ever thought of what happens after death?

4. What supernatural powers do you suppose we will have since there is an "afterlife?"

5. Have you ever experienced, or heard of someone who has experienced, the presence of angels?

6. Have you ever experienced, or heard of someone who has experienced, the presence of demons?

Destination Darkness, The End of the Other Path

In the last chapter, we saw a vivid portrayal of a white room containing either a window-like portal or a disc hologram on the floor and the earth hanging suspended in it. We also watched the two paths launching from the earth. One path led to a brilliant light and Jesus waiting to welcome us (others have had similar experiences, and have even seen other beings and people who have preceded them to the light).[5]

However, there is more to the story revealed in this experience. There was and is another path. Putting my foot upon that path, I was overwhelmed by feelings of being completely lost and alone in a black darkness that was intensifying and coming closer by the second. I felt loneliness like I'd never felt before. Though I don't know how this happened, I could, in fact, hear groans and sounds of lost people stumbling around in the dark, falling over one another, and other sounds that were horrific and repulsive beyond one's imagination.

As this darkness was quickly enveloping me, I removed my foot from the path and hurriedly placed my other foot on the path leading toward the brilliant light.

The Kingdom of Darkness

Let's attempt to come to some understanding of this darkness, this kingdom, and its king who so desperately tries to take all of us down this dark path.

Burned into my memory is the darkness that could be felt as I put my foot on its path. Just imagine what it would be like if you left your body, realized you had a new one, and then discovered there was a path before you or a tunnel in front of you. As you looked at these, it was clear by the outcome of the tunnel or path's direction (darkness or light) that you were pointed in the direction you chose to make while here on earth before this transition. This happens while on earth in this body of earthly flesh. Read on to discover what happens corresponding to our choices.

Bipolar News—Bad and Good

As has been stated before, there are two kingdoms—one of light (good) and the other of darkness (evil). There is bad news if you find yourself alive beyond death and you are on the path or pointing in the tunnel leading toward the darkness.

We will talk of the light in the next chapter, but keep reading for greater understanding of the kingdom of darkness that is in a battle for your very life and soul.

The Bible contains some descriptors of the darkness I experienced (even though only for a very short time). It uses the term "outer darkness" sometimes to describe a terrible place (Matthew 25:30). Picture being in the presence of the most amazing light and love and at the perimeter of this light is vast darkness. Here are just a few scriptures that contain appropriate words about darkness and outer darkness.

He keeps the feet of his godly ones, [i.e., those who have chosen to walk with Him] **but the wicked ones are silenced in darkness**; *for not by might shall a man prevail* (1 Samuel 2:9).

There were those who **dwelt in darkness** and in the shadow of death, prisoners in misery and chains, because they had rebelled against the words of God and spurned the counsel of the Most High [God] (Psalm 107:10).

The Darkness Described Is Overwhelming

After we look at the descriptors of the dark kingdom we will look at a professor of art explaining his experience of being drawn into the outer darkness by what seemed to be his friend's voices.

The darkness I felt from the white room was sufficient to influence me to let others know about its horrible endless conclusion. It was overwhelming my entire being, and I was only feeling the fringe edge of it from a distance.

*If I say, "Surely **the darkness will overwhelm me**, and the light around me will be night..."* (Psalms 139:11).

Multitudes Will Stumble There

Remember earlier in this book my description of hearing countless people stumbling over the unknown because of the darkness. This is a biblical concept that Solomon wrote about:

*The way of the wicked is like **darkness**; they do not know over what they **stumble*** (Proverbs 4:19).

A Place of Weeping and Gnashing of Teeth

As the realization of an eternal darkness sinks in, there are the sounds of wailing, weeping, and gnashing of teeth (the grinding one's teeth in total aguish and agony).

Jesus used this phrase in His teaching to portray the futility of the wicked who will be judged by God at the end of time:

*"For everyone who has, more shall be given, and he will have an abundance; but from the one who does not have, even what he does have shall be taken away. Throw out the worthless slave into the **outer darkness**; in that place, there will be weeping and **gnashing of teeth**"* (Matthew 25:30).

Then the king said to the servants, "Bind him

hand and foot, and throw him into the **outer darkness***; in that place there will be weeping and* **gnashing of teeth***"* (Matthew 22:13).

Note: I've included these two references for a reason. If something is stated in the sacred Scriptures it is important, but if it is mentioned multiple times, it is critically important.

You might say, your life (eternal) depends on it. Incidentally, "outer darkness" is mentioned three times in Matthew's Gospel and Jesus used the phrase "gnashing of teeth" seven times in His teaching.

Some People Love the Darkness While on Earth

The picture I've always had in my mind from that verse is someone who hears about God, spits at His feet (figuratively) and turns away to follow his or her own ambitions and selfish pursuits.

"This is the judgment, that the light has come into the world, and men [and women] loved the darkness rather than the light, for their deeds were evil" (John 3:19).

Darkness Reserved for Judgment

God created a place of outer darkness for the fallen angels who chose to follow Satan in his rebellion against God's kingdom of light. Eventually, we will not be harassed by them ever again.

For if God did not spare angels when they

*sinned [Lucifer and those who followed him], but cast them into hell and committed them to pits of darkness, **reserved for judgment** ... (2 Peter 2:4).*

*And angels who did not keep their own domain, but abandoned their proper abode, He has kept in eternal bonds under darkness for the **judgment** of the great day (Jude 1:6).*

Could the Darkness Be Hell?

If a being was exposed to the light and the amazing love of God, then find themselves in an outer darkness forever, they would burn like fire with a desire to be back in the light, love, and acceptance rather than where they had chosen.

"But I will warn you whom to fear: fear the One who, after He has killed, has authority to cast into hell; yes, I tell you, fear Him!" (Luke 12:5).

According to Wikipedia, "Hell is a place of torment and punishment in an afterlife. It is viewed by most Abrahamic traditions as punishment. Religions with a linear divine history often depict hell as an eternal destination. Religions with a cyclic history often depict hell as an intermediary period between incarnations. Typically, these traditions locate hell in another dimension or under the earth's surface and often include entrances to hell from the land of the living." (Wikipedia, 2016c)

In Jewish Rabbinic literature, and Christian and Islamic scripture, Gehenna is a destination of the wicked. This is different from the more neutral Sheol/Hades, the abode of the dead, although the King James Version of the Bible usually translates both with the Anglo-Saxon word hell.

A Professor and the Afterlife

Howard Storm was a professor of art at Northern Kentucky University when the following incident happened. He was taking students along with his wife, Beverly, on a tour of Paris' museums, when suddenly, in the afternoon, he experienced pain that he described was like being shot in the abdomen with a gun. It was excruciating. He had a duodenal hole (a leak in the small intestine). Blood was filling up his abdominal cavity. The hotel staff got a doctor to examine him and the doctor said that he needed to be hospitalized immediately.

Beverly got into the ambulance with him in Paris. And after a quick ride through the Parisian streets they made it to the hospital. He said, "I didn't know that on weekends Parisian hospitals are understaffed."

He continues, "When we got to the emergency room, they inserted a large rubber tube through my nose and down into my stomach to suction out the digestive fluids. I was being eaten alive inside by them because I had a duodenal hole.

So, from the time of perforation in the early afternoon, till around 9 o'clock I was waiting. One of the nurses came into the room; saying the doctor had gone home and the operation couldn't be performed until the next morning. "I knew I was dying! I turned to my wife Beverly who had been crying for hours, and I'd never seen her look so distressed. I told her that I loved her very, very much. I told her it was over. We said our goodbyes to each other."

Later, when talking with American doctors, he found out how serious of a problem it was. Usually a person lasts only around five hours and then death happens.

"The minutes stretched into hours that I was laying there in the emergency ... and then I was taken to another room in the hospital and, again, no doctor saw me. My whole life had been one of self-sufficient stoicism. I believed I didn't need anyone's help. I could handle anything. I could do this, I thought."

Howard had never prayed, never even thought about God, because he was convinced that there is no life after death. The following are his own words:

"I just figured that it was the end so, I said goodbye to my wife and explain that I wanted her to tell my family that I loved them. I closed my eyes. I knew that what would happen next would be the end of any kind of consciousness or existence. I knew for certain that there was no such thing as life after death, I didn't believe in God, or heaven, or hell, or any other fairytales.

"Then, I was standing up. I opened my eyes to see why was standing and I was between the hospital beds looking at my wife, trying to get her attention; trying to get the man's attention who was in the bed next to me. This has got to be a dream I thought to myself. But I knew that it wasn't. I was aware that I felt more alert, more aware, and more alive than I'd ever felt in my entire life.

"As I bent over to look at the face of the body in the bed next to my wife, I was horrified to see the resemblance that it had to my own face. Just then, off in the distance, outside the room in the hallway, I heard voices calling me, 'Howard, Howard.' They were pleasant voices, male and female, young and old, calling to me in English. This was unusual because all the hospital staff spoke French."

"Come out here," they said, "let's go, hurry up. We've been waiting for you a long time." "I can't," I said, "I'm sick. Something's the matter with me; something's wrong in here. I need an operation, I am very sick!" "We can get you fixed up," they said, "If you hurry up, don't you want to get better? Don't you want help?"

He went into the hallway to follow them to what he supposed was the surgery room.

"I quickly realized the further I followed these people, that I was not in the hospital anymore. This great hallway had gotten darker and darker and darker. The people stayed further away so that I could not see them clearly. How could this hospital hallway be so long? No uphill or downhill, but sometimes I had the strange feeling that we might be subtly descending.

"I also couldn't make out how much time was passing. There was a profound sense of timelessness. Whoever these beings were, it became increasingly clear to me that they were deceiving me. The longer I stayed with them, the further away escape would be. It was like I was being forced by a mob of unfeeling people toward some unknown destination in the encroaching darkness. Then they began shouting and hurling insults at me, demanding that I hurry along. The more miserable I became, the more enjoyment they derived from the distress.[6]

"For a long time, I'd been walking with my gaze down to watch my step. When I looked around I was completely horrified to discover that we were in complete darkness. I told them I would go no farther, to leave me alone, and that they were a bunch of liars. I could feel their breath on me as they shouted and snarled insults. Then they begin to push and shove me about and I begin to fight back. A wild frenzy of taunting, screaming, and hitting ensued. I fought like a wild man. As I swung and kicked at them, they bit and tore back at me. All the while it was obvious that they were having great fun. Even though I couldn't see anything in the darkness, I was aware that there were dozens or even hundreds of them all around me and all over me. My attempts to fight back only provoked greater merriment. As I continued to defend myself, I was aware that they weren't in any hurry to annihilate me. They were playing with me just like a cat plays with a mouse. Every new assault brought howls of cacophonous laughter. They began to tear off pieces of my flesh. To my horror, I realize that I was being taken apart and eaten alive, methodically, slowly, so that their entertainment would last long as possible."[7]

"Eventually I became too badly torn up and too broken to resist. Most of them gave up tormenting me because I was no longer amusing, but a few still picked and gnawed at me and ridiculed me for no longer being amusing. I had been torn apart. In that wretched state, I lay there in the darkness.

"I haven't described everything that happened. There are things that I don't care to remember. In fact, much that occurred was simply too gruesome and disturbing to recall. I've spent years trying to suppress a lot of it. After the experience, whenever I did remember those details, I would become traumatized."

Then Howard goes on to say, "I was alone, destroyed, and yet painfully alive in this revolting horrible place. I had no idea where I was. At first, when I was walking with these beings, I thought we were in some foggy part of the hospital. Now, I didn't know if I was even in the world. I was alone in that darkness for time without measure. I thought about what I had done. All my life I had thought that hard work was what counted. My life was devoted to building a monument to my ego. My family, my sculptures, my painting, my house, my gardens, my little fame, my illusions of power, were all an extension of my ego."

Storm goes on to say, "How ironic it was to end

up in the sewer of the universe with people who fed off the pain of others! I had had little genuine compassion for others. It dawned on me that I was not unlike these miserable creatures that tormented me. I viewed people who were religious with contempt. I thought they believed in fairy tales because they couldn't cope with the harsh reality of life.

In a nutshell, this is the description of his life. "I was in control of my life. I believed in being a law-abiding citizen and that you should avoid going to jail at all costs. I didn't rob banks or murder anyone. I lived within the law of the land and obeyed the unwritten rules of civility. Wasn't this sufficient for a good life?

The rugged individualism that I have learned from my father, my schooling, and my American culture was my religion. Why would I need to believe in a higher power? Who would put the needs of others ahead of their own needs? You must watch your own back always. Life is every man for himself. The one who dies with the most toys wins. Compassion is for the weak. If you don't take care of yourself, nobody else will.

"I didn't believe in life after death. When you died, it was like having a switch turned off that was it, the end of your existence, finished, just darkness. Now I was in that darkness, beyond life, and it was hell. Once the beings retreated, I found myself laying on the ground; completely alone, painfully alive, and intensely aware of this horrible place."[8]

I have shared Howard's experience because there may be some of you who read this, who, like him, don't think there's a real place for people who end up on the path of darkness. We will continue with his experience a little later. But, for now, suffice it to know that this believer in nothing after death found a different set of events than he had expected.

Other Things Could Influence Us Toward the Darkness

Jesus spoke at least one time of hell like being in prison. Here are some of the main ways to get into this prison. See the following references for this important principle.

• Not forgiving others.

Most of us, if not all, know what has been called the Lord's prayer. You know, the passage of Scripture that starts with: "Our Father who art in heaven," but most people don't realize the importance and significance given to forgiveness in the Lord's prayer. Here it is in its entirety:

> Our Father who is in heaven, hallowed be Your name. Your kingdom come. Your will be done, On earth as it is in heaven. Give us this day our daily bread. **And forgive us our debts, as we also have forgiven our debtors.** And do not lead us into temptation, but deliver us from evil. [For yours is the kingdom and the power and the glory forever. Amen.] (Matthew 6:9-13)

I'm reminded of a time when I was speaking in a meeting, expounding on forgiveness. A young man in the meeting lost his composure as he was telling us that he would never, ever forgive his father. As we talked with him and prayed for him later, he forgave his father. And he stated that it felt like thousands of pounds just rolled from his shoulders.

Another incident happened in a Chinese church I was speaking at. There was an older Chinese man who was sitting near the back of the church. As I was teaching on forgiveness, I could tell he was not comfortable. Finally, he raised his hand and in a very anxious voice said, "Are you saying that I need to forgive the Japanese people?" To which I said, "It wasn't me who said it."

Then we read the Scripture from Matthew six and I asked him who had spoken those words? He said, "Jesus spoke those words." So, I asked him, "Who is Jesus?" He stated, "Jesus is God, the Son." Then I said, "God says that we need to forgive everybody, not because they deserve it."

After struggling for a while with this concept, the man came forward and prayed with me, picturing all the Japanese people in front of him and he spoke out his forgiveness for all the Japanese people and everything they've done to the Chinese people (especially during World War II). An amazing thing happened! He was released to such a degree that he fell upon the floor and looked kind of like a fish out of water that was bouncing around. I had never seen anything so wonderful, when he stood up again he was a changed person. Forgiveness had literally changed his life. Jesus went on to say in that same chapter:

"For if you forgive others for their transgressions, your heavenly father will also forgive you. But if you do not forgive others, then your Father will not forgive you your transgressions" (Matthew 6:14).

Notice in this prayer that Jesus is teaching His disciples and us how to pray; in verse 12 He says, "Forgive us our debts (sins) as we forgive our debtors (those who have sinned against us)." When He said the word "as," the meaning would be something like this—Oh, God, please forgive me in the same way that I forgive those whom I perceive have sinned against me. If we have not forgiven yet and prayed that God would forgive us in exactly that same way, what would be the outcome? So, if we don't forgive, could this possibly be one of hell's means to get us to join the group there? I don't know, but I have decided to forgive everyone just to be on the safe side!

• Speaking against the Holy Spirit.

Jesus said, "Therefore I say to you, any sin and blasphemy shall be forgiven people but blasphemy against the Spirit shall not be forgiven. Whoever speaks a word against the Son of Man [Jesus], it shall be forgiven him; but whoever speaks against the Holy Spirit, it shall not be forgiven him, either in this age or in the age to come" (Matthew 12:31).

Note: the main reason that Jesus said these words so strongly was an experience that just preceded them. There was a demon possessed man who was blind and mute and he was brought to Jesus, and He healed him, so that the mute man spoke and saw. All the crowds were quite amazed and they were saying *"This man cannot be the son of David [a reference to the Messiah], can he?"* But when the Pharisees heard this, they said, *"This man cast out demons only by Beelzebul the ruler of the demons"* (Matthew 12:24).

There was a reason that this was referred to as speaking against the Holy Spirit. Jesus was not doing the miracles or casting out demons by His own power, but by the Holy Spirit's power. He had left His glory and possibly His authority in heaven when He became a man. Ironically, Jesus, who was God in human form, was doing the work of God and people said it was by Beelzebul (a term for Satan that means "lord of the flies" or "god of the dung hill").

Jesus was and is forever the Son of God—first He was in heaven, then He came to earth, and then He returned to heaven again.

And the Word became flesh and dwelt among us, and we saw His glory, glory as of only begotten from the Father, full of grace and truth (John 1:14).

But when the fullness of the time came,

God sent forth His Son, born of a woman, born under the Law, so that He might redeem those who were under the Law, that we might receive the adoptions as sons (Galatians 4:4-5).

Have this attitude in yourselves which was also in Christ Jesus, who, although He existed in the form of God, did not regard equality with God a thing to be grasped, but emptied Himself, taking the form of a bond-servant, and being made in the likeness of men. Being found in appearance as a man, He humbled Himself by becoming obedient to the point of death, even death on a cross. For this reason also, God highly exalted Him, and bestowed on Him the name which is above every name, so that at the name of Jesus every knee will bow, of those who are in heaven and on earth and under the earth, and that every tongue will confess that Jesus Christ is Lord, to the glory of God the Father (Philippians 2:5-11).

Then Jesus arrived from Galilee at the Jordan coming to John, to be baptized by him. But John tried to prevent Him, saying, "I have need to be baptized by You, and do You come to me?" But Jesus answering said to him, "Permit it at this time; for in this way it is fitting for to fulfill all righteousness." Then he permitted Him. After being baptized, Jesus came up immediately from the water; and behold, the heavens were opened, and he saw the **Spirit of God** *descending as* *a dove and lighting on Him, and behold, a voice out of the heavens said, "This is My beloved Son, in whom I am well-pleased"* (Matthew 3:13-17).

We see that Jesus, being fully human, relied upon the Holy Spirit, though He certainly was and is God, who came to earth. Nevertheless, from the above scriptures we realize, He was not operating as God while in human form on the earth, but relied upon the Spirit of God, the Holy Spirit to lead, empower Him, and work through Him.

So, these Jewish leaders who were speaking against the power with which Jesus was casting out demons were blaspheming the Holy Spirit, calling Him the devil. Again, I don't know if one would end up in hell for doing this, but, as strong as Jesus' admonition was, I would not test out the theory by calling anything done by the Holy Spirit a work of the devil!

• **Rejecting Christ's provision for sin.**

Lastly, but most importantly, we need to consider the claims that Jesus made about Himself. We need to make an informed decision about Him and we need to accept the way that God planned for us to have our sins erased. The word "sin" is not a term that we know much about in these days. By sin it is meant the things that we've done wrong knowingly, those things, either what we've said or not said, done or not done, that the Word of God and our conscience tells us are wrong.

In almost every culture there are cultural norms of behavior and what is considered right and wrong. The biblical culture is no exception. The more we know of this culture, the more we know what pleases God and what displeases God. If something we do displeases God, it more than likely is a sin. We will continue with a short, simple way to make sure we are forgiven in Chapter 8, but, for now, read on to understand the amazing kingdom of light and love awaiting us!

This Place of Darkness Was Not Created for Humans

As far as I can understand, hell, or the outer darkness, was not created for and is not intended for humans. This everlasting place of outer darkness and continual torment was created for Satan and the demons (fallen angels) who chose to rebel against God's kingdom (Matthew 25:41).

For Humans, Hell Is a Choice

"From those who leave the paths of uprightness to walk in the ways of darkness" (Proverbs 2:13). Intentionally staying away from God and His plan will put one on the path to darkness, while choosing His plan and way will put one on the path to unimaginable light, love, and life.

The fact that there is a kingdom indicates that there must be a king. A kingdom is a king's domain (the boundaries wherein a king rules). So, the kingdom of God is His authority, rulership, or jurisdiction. The same is true for Satan's kingdom of darkness. Paul wrote about these two kingdoms, *"For He rescued us from **the domain of darkness**, and transferred us to the **kingdom of His beloved Son**, in whom we have redemption, the forgiveness of sins"* (Colossians 1:13-14).

How, when, where, why, and who is the present discussion. Again, the author is writing from 2,000 years of documentation, theory, and reality as well as the reality of his own experiences.

Who Is this King of Darkness?

As stated before, it is not Darth Vader or some other fictional character. This king has been called many names in many cultures: (Note: other names for him have been derived from mythological and cultural references.)

- O-Yama—Japanese (Lord of Death).
- Beelzebul—(Beelzebub NKJV, Lord of the Flies)—Matthew 10:25.
- Yen-lo-Wang—Chinese (Ruler of Hell).
- Lucifer—(Light Bearer)—Isaiah 14:12.
- Satan—(Slanderer)—Revelation 12:9.
- Devil—(False Accuser)—Revelation 12:9.
- Adversary—(One Who Opposes or Attacks)—1 Peter 5:8.
- The Serpent—Genesis 3:1, Revelation 12:9.
- The Great Red Dragon—Revelation 12:3.

- Belial (Worthless, Lawless Fellow)—
  2 Corinthians 6:15.

- Abaddon/Apollyon (Destroyer)—
  Revelation 9:11.

- Prince of this World—John 12:31,
  John 16:11.

- Prince of the Power of the Air—
  Ephesians 2:2.

- Prince/Chief of the Devils—Matthew 9:34,
  Luke 11:15.

- God of this World—2 Corinthians 4:4.

- The Thief (One Who Steals, Kills, and
  Destroys)—John 10:10.

- The Enemy—Matthew 13:39.

- The Tempter—Matthew 4:3.

- The Evil/Wicked One—John 17:15,
  1 John 2:13-14.

- Murderer—John 8:44.

- Liar/Father of Lies—John 8:44.

- Deceiver—Revelation 12:9; 20:3, 8, 10.

- The Wolf—John 10:12.

- A Roaring Lion—1 Peter 5:8.

- Fowler (Bird Catcher)—Psalms 91:3; 124:7.

So, What Happened to Howard Storm?

Before you read further, let's finish Howard

Storm's experience. Remember the Ph. D. art professor, who was lured into the hallway from his deathbed? His story continues:

"As I lay on the ground, my tormentors swarming around me, a voice emerged from my chest. It sounded like my voice, but it wasn't my thoughts. The voice that sounded like my voice but wasn't said, 'Pray to God.' I remember thinking, Why? What a stupid idea. That doesn't work. What a cop-out. Lying here in the darkness surrounded by hideous creatures, I don't even believe in God. This is utterly hopeless, and I am beyond any possible help whether I believe in God or not. I don't pray, period!

"A second time, the voice spoke to me, 'Pray to God.' Pray, How? Pray what? I hadn't prayed any time in my entire adult life. I didn't know how to pray. I wouldn't know what right words to say even if I did pray. I can't pray! And then the voice said it again, 'Pray to God.' As a child, I watched adults pray. I tried to remember the prayers from my childhood experiences at Sunday School. What could I remember. I remembered a few lines—a jumble from the twenty-third Psalm, the Star-Spangled Banner, the Lord's Prayer, and God Bless America.

"Yea, though I walk through the valley of the shadow of death, I will fear no evil, for Thou art with me. Mine eyes have seen the glory of the coming of the Lord. Deliver us from evil. One nation under God. God bless America.

"To my amazement, I found that the cruel,

merciless beings tearing the life out of me were incited to rage by my ragtag prayer. It was as if I were throwing boiling oil on them. They screamed at me, saying, 'There is no God! Who do you think you're talking to? Nobody can hear you! Now we're really going to hurt you.'

"They spoke in the most obscene language; worse than any blasphemy said on earth, but at the same time they were backing away from me. I realized that saying things about God was driving them away. I became a little more forceful, 'Yea, though I walk through the valley of the shadow of death, God is going to get you. Leave me alone, the Lord is my shepherd and one nation under God, etc.'

"I didn't believe in a life after death. When you died, it was like having the switch turned off. That was it, the end of your existence, finished, just darkness. Now I was in that darkness, beyond life, and it was hell.

"I knew then that this was the absolute end of my existence in the world, and it was more horrible than anything I could possibly have imagined. It would have been much better to die in the hospital than live in this despicable garbage heap. I felt like a match whose flame had been spent and the ember was slowly dying away to nothing. Little strength was left to resist becoming a creature gnashing his teeth in the outer darkness. I wasn't far from becoming like one of my own tormentors for all eternity."[9]

In Howard's case, he experienced an amazing thing.

"Then for the first time in my adult life a very old tune from childhood started going through my head. It was my voice, but it sounded like a little boy singing the same line over and over again. The child that I had once been was singing full of innocence, trust, and hope. "Jesus loves me, da, da, da ... " There was only that little bit of the tune and those few words that I could remember. We had sung those words in Sunday School when I was a child."[10]

"I desperately needed someone to love me, someone to know I was alive. A ray of hope began to dawn in me, a belief that there really was something greater out there. For the first time in my adult life I wanted it to be true that Jesus loved me. I didn't know how to express what I wanted and needed, but with every bit of my last ounce of strength, I yelled out into the darkness, 'Jesus, save me.' I yelled that from the core of my being with all the energy I had left. I have never meant anything more strongly in my life.

"Far off in the darkness I saw a pinpoint of light like the faintest star in the sky. I wondered why I hadn't seen it before. The star was rapidly getting brighter and brighter. At first I thought it might be something, not someone. It was moving toward me at an alarming rate. As it came closer, I realized that I was right in its path and I might be consumed by its brilliance. I couldn't take my eyes off it; the light was more intense and more beautiful than anything I had ever seen."[11]

Howard explained that he was then taken a long way at an incredible speed and, in his words:

"Off in the distance far, far away, I saw a vast area of illumination that looked like a galaxy. In the center was an enormously bright concentration of light. Outside the center, countless millions of spheres of light were flying about, entering and leaving that great concentration of light at the center. This was comparable to seeing the sky at night on the top of a mountain with the stars so abundant that they almost touch one another. These "stars" were all in motion in relation to the center. They were moving toward or away from the brilliant white center of the universe.

"As we approached, still a vast distance away, I was permeated with tangible intense feelings and thoughts of love. While moving toward the presence of the great light, center of all being, The One, I was beyond thought. It is not possible to articulate what occurred. Simply, I knew that God loved me, that God loved creation, that God is love. This experience of love totally changed my life from the inside out. No matter what happened, I would always know that God loved me."[12]

A Short Ending to the Long Experience

After long conversations with angels, and with Jesus, Howard found himself back in the hospital. He said, "I was back in the bed that I left earlier.

The pain I suffered before this experience had returned with a vengeance, especially since I had come from ecstasy only to return suddenly to this agony. Immediately, several nurses and orderlies came into the room and sent Beverly out, against turbulent protests. They had come to prepare me for the operation that I had long awaited. It was now past 9 o'clock at night and they announced that a doctor had arrived to do the surgery.

As I was being pushed on the gurney down the hall, Beverly came alongside and grabbed my hand. I told her that everything was going to be fine. I was confident because I knew that I had God and the angels on my side, and that my life was not at an end just now because they had sent me back for a second chance. As soon as we arrived in the operating area, I was given an injection and lost consciousness."

Howard indeed made it through the surgery, and sooner than thought, was able to fly back to the USA. In his words, "During this time of recovery, I thought, studied, and prayed. My life had been lost and given back. Physically and spiritually I was born again. This rocked the foundations of all that I had previously believed, demanding that my entire life be rebuilt."

And finally, Howard says, "I received a new life because I confessed and was forgiven. How simple it is and how much people resist doing it."

To be forgiven is to be given a second chance, given new life. We need only to make an honest confession and ask to be forgiven to have a new beginning. Love, hope, faith, and joy await us when we give it all over to God.

My own thoughts run along the same line as Howard's. When I began telling my story, I didn't want to offend anyone. This caused me to be vague about certain things I've been told. After speaking to so many groups that have included mainline Christians, Hindus, Mormons, agnostics, Pentecostals, Jews, new agers, cynics, doctors, scientists, and others, I realize that it is better just to tell it unvarnished and let them decide for themselves what relevance it has to their life. My responsibility is to be faithful to the truth as it has been revealed to me by God and according to my understanding.

I pray that you will find my story, as well as Howard's, to be consistent with the Gospels of Matthew, Mark, Luke, and John. I suggest that you look at the story of the Prodigal Son in the Gospel of Luke 15:11-32; this is similar to Howard's story.

Maurice Rawling's Research

A close friend, Carol, related the following:

"While working at Hawthorne Community Hospital in the 1980's, we started a lunch time Book/Bible study for any employees who wanted to attend. During that time, one of the books that we discussed was entitled, *Beyond Death's Door* by Maurice Rawlings.

"Rawlings was a non-believing cardiologist who experienced, first hand, a challenge to his belief that there was nothing beyond this life. He was working on one of the occasional resuscitations where as long as cardiac compressions are continued, the patient is alert, oriented, and able to talk to those working to save their life. Dr. Rawling's patient, who flatlined every time chest compressions were stopped, begged him not to let him die as he said he was going to hell. This put extreme pressure on the medical staff to continue the resuscitation and not call the code.

"After that experience, Rawlings started inter-viewing patients who had been resuscitated. He found that if he interviewed them immediately after they were resuscitated, he got two different stories; one of seeing the light, going to heaven, seeing other believers who had gone before them, talking to the Lord, and there being a reason that they had to go back, the other story was of going to hell, seeing demons, seeing the lake of fire and experiencing terrifying things. He found that if he waited even twenty-four hours or a week after a resuscitation to interview patients, he got only the story of going to heaven or nothing at all. He deducted from this that the experience of going to hell was so terrifying that within a day or a week, patients pushed that experience into their subconscious mind as they were unable to deal with it. This led Rawlings to become a Christian, accept the Lord, and publish his book with the many interviews that had led him to a life changing decision.

"After discussing this book, and making many of the hospital staff aware of this story, we found that we had varied responses to its content. It was definitely a challenging idea for marginal believers, and it met with hostility from those who felt that the life of a patient hanging in the balance was only their responsibility. Some of the medical staff, who had not confirmed in their own life that there was a God and that Jesus was Lord and Savior, struggled in acceptance of the idea that the Lord had the final say as to when a person died.

"However, God was a faithful teacher, and sent us a rash of patients who required resuscitation. Many of those who came through the ER doors went on to meet their Maker despite all the heroic efforts of the well-trained staff, but then we got a patient named Joe (named changed to protect patient privacy).

"Joe came into the ER in full cardiac arrest. We resuscitated him, and he was successfully sent to the Cardiac Intensive Care Unit. While in CICU, Joe arrested another fourteen times. After the last one of those middle-of-the-night arrests and resuscitations, I noticed that Joe looked terrified. He was ghost white, diaphoretic, and had the look of sheer terror in his eyes. I said to him, 'Joe, what are you thinking, you look scared to death?'

"He then related to me that during his arrest, he experienced going to hell, seeing demons grabbing out at him, and encountered Satan himself trying to drag him down to the pit and the lake of fire for eternity. He was genuinely terrified. I prayed with him, and later brought him the *Beyond Death's Door* book which he read.

"After discussion of the book and many prayers, Joe accepted the Lord. He then went on to Harbor General Hospital where he had successful open-heart surgery with a quadruple bypass graft. He later returned to our hospital to tell his story, and to thank us for not giving up on him and for saving his life.

"Shortly after Joe's story had been circulated throughout the hospital, we got another full arrest patient who was brought into our ER by the paramedics. This patient was a big kingpin in the mafia in Hawthorne. While we were working on his resuscitation, periodically as is common, we would stop in order to see if an effectual cardiac rhythm had been restored. During these pauses in resuscitation, a blood-curdling scream, as if from beyond the grave, shrieked out of him. It was a scream that you never forget, and it stood the hair on the back of your neck on end. The atmosphere in the ER grew increasingly tense as with each pause we were subjected to another blood-curdling shriek.

"Everyone on the team was uneasy and whispering to one another, 'Do you think he's going to hell?' Despite all our well-trained resuscitation efforts, that patient met his demise."

Note: these are only a few cases out of many hundreds that have been researched. These cases have been included so the reader might understand that if we believe that there is an afterlife or not, or whether or not we believe there's a dark side and a light side, does not change the reality of these things. If you are on the path of darkness, your belief system here on this earth will be radically altered at the point of death, even as Howard's was.

Chapter 7: Q & A

1. What things have you read about that happen to people when they die?

2. Why would certain people find themselves on the path to darkness after they die?

3. Are there any descriptions of the darkness that stand out in your memory?

4. Why is forgiveness so very important?

5. Why is speaking against God's Holy Spirit so dangerous?

6. What are the seeming consequences of doing this?

7. What happens to one who rejects Christ's provision for sin?

8. Please explain the statement: "The darkness was not created for humans."

In the next chapter, we will discuss the ultimate destination of the path/tunnel, which is light.

The Place of Intense, Stunning Light

From researching others who've studied and tried to understand NDEs, the following has been discovered:

- People have NDEs while they are brain-dead.

In some cases researched, those who have been long enough without oxygen to be "brain dead" have experiences NDEs and have come back to tell about it.[13]

- Many people born blind can see during NDEs.[14]

- Out-of-body perceptions during NDEs have been verified.

Note: this is a very important factor, or, should we say, "fact." If there were no verification of these experiences, we could attribute them to the mind, or a chemical change at the point of death, etc., but with verification of so many experiences—there is NO DOUBT as to their authenticity.

The replication study of Dr. Raymond Moody's book, *"Life After Life,"* was done by Dr. Kenneth Ring. Dr. Moody's research findings have been confirmed. By this, it is understood that Dr. Ring found that the same experiences were happening enough to prove that the earlier conclusions by Dr. Moody's research were accurate. This is important. It is the foundation on which the rest of NDE research stands.

Here are only a few of Dr. Ring's research conclusions:

- NDEs happen to all types of people: all races, genders, ages, education levels, marital status, and social class. Everybody dies!

- Religious orientation doesn't matter.

- It is also noteworthy that the description of the God/Man in a high percentage of the NDEs is quite similar—and describes what the Bible portrays so accurately of description of the Son of Man (Jesus).

- People are convinced of the reality of their NDE experiences. In my opinion, this is because it really happened.

- Drugs do not appear to be a factor, administration of drugs or attempts to change brain chemistry have not produced effects of near-death or out-of-the-body experiences.

- NDEs often involve seeming supernatural sensory perception, such as "zoom vision." The feeling of being fully alive is reported by a good percentage of people who have had NDEs.

- Most people lose the fear of death and gain a positive perception of life after an NDE.

  Note: this all depends on where (directionally) the person is headed. If the path or end of the tunnel is darkness, then there is either a thought that at the end is "nothingness," or a major panic attack at what was perceived as waiting for them in this abysmal end. But, if the end of the path or tunnel is light, then there is a euphoric feeling and experience.

- People's lives are typically transformed after having an NDE. After such an awareness that life goes on in a new supernatural body. There is a newly heightened awareness that every day is a preparatory day for eternity.

People make statements like, "I live each day as if it were my last here on earth and look forward to my new body." We will all die, per the studies we've been reading, but death of the exterior only allows release of the interior (soul and spirit) of a person. This is great news to all of us! "When I was seeing myself out of my body, it was because it was really happening." When people who are experiencing death leave the body, it is not hallucination, but rather, it is fact that they are "leaving their body."

Just imagine what you would feel like if you left your body, and realized you had a new one and then discovered there were two paths or tunnels in front of you. As you looked at these, it was clear that the outcome of the tunnel or path's direction was a direct result of the choices you made while on earth. If one thinks about it, it is kind of like having an invisible path while here are on earth that continues to the ultimate destination when a person "passes on." They are just continuing the path of their choices.

The paths and their destinations that I saw, and that I've since gained insight into through research, are very real and end up in exact opposite places. One is a terrible place reserved for those who participate in the kingdom of darkness, along with the fallen angels and Satan himself, who do not want to change while on earth. The other path leads to a wonderful place reserved for those that participate in the kingdom of light while here. People, knowingly or unknowingly, make choices that affect their eternal destiny while they live on this earth. Decisions determine our destiny. Destiny is not a matter of chance; it's a matter of choice!

Dr. Bruce Graysen documented perhaps one of the most compelling examples of a person who had an NDE and observed events while outside of his body which were later verified by others. The only way that these events could have been observed by the experiencer was if he was literally outside of his body. He tells the story of Al Sullivan, a fifty-five-year-old truck driver who was undergoing triple by-pass surgery in 1988 when he had a powerful NDE. It included an encounter with his deceased mother and brother-in-law, who told Al to go back to tell one of his neighbors that their son, a victim of lymphoma, would live. Furthermore, during the NDE, Sullivan accurately noticed the surgeon, Dr.

Hiroyoshi Takata, operating on him was "flapping his arms as if trying to fly" with his hands in his armpits. When he came back to his body after the surgery was over, Sullivan's cardiologist was startled that Sullivan could describe Dr. Takata's habit of arm flapping. It was Dr. Takata's idiosyncratic method of keeping his hands sterile and pointing out to surgical instruments and giving instructions to his surgical staff.[15]

In his research, Dr. Ring gives documentation providing the solid evidence of thirty-one cases in which blind people reported visually accurate information obtained during their NDEs.

Our New Body

Many others have experienced similar aware-ness as I did, that we were no longer in the same body and were seeing and feeling more fully alive; as if we were less than completely alive here on earth. The senses have a heightened awareness and sensitivity.

Similar Experiences

With the revolution in medical procedures and the advancements that have happened over the years, we have seen increasing NDEs and out-of-body experiences. And, though not all stories are alike, those who have experienced them, like me, are having many, many similar things to share.

The new body we morph into has amazing visual perception. When I saw Jesus, because of the distance between He and me, I did not recognize

Him at first. But at the mere thought, I wonder what He looks like? It was like I had zoom lenses in my new eyes. I could zoom in and see His facial features. A Jewish looking man, not terribly handsome, with a dark brown, very well-groomed beard. His eyes were like burning flames of fire inside them just as they are described in Revelation 1:14. When He looked at me, there was an overwhelming love, acceptance, and patience even though I knew that He knew everything I had ever done—the good and the bad.

This chapter (eight) and chapter nine will not have Q & A like the other chapters. We have provided the answers right after the questions. You may have different answers, but again, we want to understand as much as possible on this adventure. So, while we may have our own opinions of the answers, please let's read those provided to get a more enlightened perspective.

Questions: Is there a heaven? What is heaven like and where is it? What do you think?

Answers: Yes, there is a place called heaven. We don't know absolutely if anyone living has seen it in its fullness, stayed there, and could communicate back to tell us what it is like. However, one who is documented in the Bible, John (in the Book of Revelation) was taken into heaven and has written what he saw and heard. We also have statements from those who have been on heaven's outskirts via NDEs or seen visions of it. Therefore, we can see glimpses of what could be in store for us and what our new bodies will be capable of. Yes, there is a heaven. What most people call "heaven" is an eternal city which the Bible calls the "New Jerusalem." It is spectacular. As a sampling, here is what heaven will look like. Just picture the following descriptions in your mind's eye.[16]

Description of Heaven

According to the Book of Revelation, written by John the Apostle, New Jerusalem is made of "pure gold, like clear glass" and its "brilliance [is] like a very costly stone, as a stone of crystal-clear jasper." The streets of the city are also made of "pure gold, like transparent glass." The base of the city is laid out in a square and surrounded by a wall made of jasper stone. It says in Revelation 21:16 that the height, length, and width are of equal dimensions— as were the Holy of Holies in the Tabernacle and in Solomon's Temple—and they measure 12,000 furlongs (which is approximately 1,500 miles).

John writes that the wall is 144 cubits, which is assumed to be the width since the length is mentioned previously (144 cubits are about equal to sixty-five meters, or seventy-two yards). It is important to note that twelve is the square root of 144. The number twelve was very important to early Jews and Christians, representing the Twelve Tribes of Israel and Twelve Apostles of Jesus Christ. The four sides of the city represent the four cardinal directions (North, South, East, and West.) In this way, New Jerusalem was thought of as an inclusive place, with gates accepting all of the Twelve Tribes of Israel from all corners of the earth.

There is no temple building in the New Jerusalem. God and Jesus the Lamb are the city's temple, since they are worshiped everywhere and their presence permeates the city. Revelation 22 goes on to describe a river of the water of life that flows down the middle of the great street of the city from the Throne of God.

The Tree of Life grows in the middle of this street and on either side, or in the middle of the street and on either side of the river. The tree bears twelve fruits, or kinds of fruits, and yields its fruit monthly. According to John, "The leaves of the tree were for the healing of the nations." This inclusion of the Tree of Life in the New Jerusalem connects back to the Garden of Eden, a restoration of what Adam and Eve lost. The fruit the tree bears produces eternal life in those who partake of it (Genesis 3:22).

John states that the New Jerusalem will be free of sin. The servants of God will experience complete union with God, be like Him in every way, and "His name will be on their foreheads." Night will no longer fall, and the inhabitants of the city will "need [no] lamp nor light of the sun, for the Lord God gives them light." John ends his account of the New Jerusalem by stressing its eternal nature: "And they shall reign forever and ever."[17]

However, the Real Beauty of Heaven Is This

And I heard a loud voice from heaven saying,

"Behold, the tabernacle of God is with men, and he will dwell with them, and they shall be his people. God himself will be with them and be their God. And God will wipe away every tear from their eyes; there shall be no more death, nor sorrow, nor crying. There shall be no more pain, for the former things have passed away." Then he who sat on the throne said, "Behold, I make all things new" (Revelation 21:3-5, NKJV).

Heaven belongs to Jesus. He created it. *"For by him all things were created, in heaven and on earth, visible and invisible ... all things were created by Him"* (Colossians 1:16). Based on what we have just discovered, it will be helpful to see what Jesus said about how a person gets to heaven.

A leader from the Jewish Sanhedrin, Nicodemus, spoke to Jesus at night:

*Now there was a man of the Pharisees, named Nicodemus, a ruler of the Jews; this man came to Jesus by night and said to Him, "Rabbi, we know that You have come from God as a teacher; for no one can do these signs that You do unless God is with him." Jesus answered and said to him, "Truly, truly, I say to you, **unless one is born again he cannot see the kingdom of God.** Nicodemus said to Him, "How can a man be born when he is old? He cannot enter a second time into his mother's womb and be born, can he?" Jesus answered, "Truly, truly, I say to you,* *unless one is born of water and the Spirit he cannot enter into the kingdom of God. That which is born of the flesh is flesh, and that which is born of the Spirit is spirit. Do not be amazed that I said to you, 'You must be born again'"* (John 3:1-7).

Born of Water

What did and does it mean to be "born of water?" It is to be born as a human being in the natural way. We all have been born on the earth through water. The amniotic fluid which surrounds the unborn baby flushes from the womb (the water breaks forth) just prior to the point of birth—many believe that this is what Jesus meant by being "born of water." It also could refer to a "spiritual cleansing" at the time of Jesus, or, perhaps it was the combination of both.

Born of the Spirit—Born Again

Being "born of the Spirit" refers to a spiritual re-birth that happens when we accept Jesus as our Lord and Savior (the salvation experience, Romans 10:9-10). Ray Stedman, famous speaker/author described this experience, "Unless one is born again he cannot see the kingdom of God." A new birth is essential to enter God's kingdom. John uses a very interesting word here that is translated "anew," or "again." It is the Greek word for another, which has three meanings:

- It means "again," or "to do it a second time."

- It also means "to begin radically, completely, a new beginning."

- It also means "from above," and it is used in that sense in other places in Scripture. It signifies that God must do this. In other words, it is a supernatural work of God not a superhuman work of man (John 1:12-13).

The Christian understanding of this word includes all three of those meanings. It is speaking of something radical, a new beginning. It is a second birth, but it comes from above. It is God that does it, not man; and it results in a new creation, a new beginning. (Stedman, 1983)

> *Therefore if anyone is in Christ, he is a **new creature**; the old things passed away; behold, new things have come* (2 Corinthians 5:17).

Another term synonymous with being "born again" that is used by theologians is "regeneration." Regeneration is the sovereign act of God whereby we are made new creatures.

> *But when the kindness of God our Savior and His love for mankind appeared, **He saved us**, not on the basis of deeds which we have done in righteousness, but according to His mercy, **by the washing of regeneration and renewing by the Holy Spirit**, whom He poured out upon us richly through Jesus Christ our Savior* (Titus 3:4-6).

Notice regeneration is not merely the improvement of the old, Adamic, fallen nature, but the impartation of a new, divine, Christ-like nature (2 Peter 1:4).

Regarding heaven, it is our decision now whether to respond to Jesus and accept His free gift of eternal life. Jesus said, *"For this is the will of my Father, that everyone who beholds the Son and believes in Him will have eternal life, and I Myself will raise him up on the last day"* (John 6:40). We're told in Scripture that in heaven there will be a multitude of people from every tribe, language, people group and nation who will have eternal life because of their faith in Jesus.

What Does It Mean to Believe in Him?

It does not mean merely believing things about Jesus. There is a difference between your believing that Barack Obama was president of the United States in 2016 versus knowing him personally. In the same way, you might believe Jesus is God, without ever inviting Him into your life.

Here is a powerful statistic, there are 637 Bible verses containing the word "Heaven." HEAVEN IS A GIVEN IN THE BIBLE! It is understood as a fact and a reality.

We Are Still on an Adventure!

Let's keep going. Follow on—we are on an adventure; and it gets more and more exciting as we discover new things together! Since there is seemingly a real heaven, how do we get there? Perhaps you still are not sure you want to go there. After many years of research on this subject, this is what I've found, there is a simple, non-complicated entrance gate. And, trust me, you do want to go there. Later, we will discuss what is the simplest way to know for sure that you and I will get to heaven and be accepted by God and be welcomed in His presence for all eternity.

Dumb Ways to Die

I once heard Rick Warren, author of *The Purpose Driven Life*, also my pastor for many years, say, "High-pressure invitations are sometimes counter-productive." While that is true, our world and our eternal future are hanging in a balance between light and darkness—forever! On the one path is a fulfilled life of joy, peace, and unimaginable love and a place that is equally indescribable. The other path is the most miserable eternal existence we can't and don't want to imagine—even worse than any movie's depiction of a demon-infested hell. And, either pathway we choose, our life goes on forever!

I am not standing on a street corner and yelling at you to "turn or burn!" But, I am so convinced of the reality of the spiritual life with Jesus that I am sincerely asking and passionately calling to you to consider what has been written.

I urge you to finish reading this book with an open mind, and I offer you an open an invitation to continue this spiritual adventure.

From the scriptures we have studied together in this book, from the historical records we have compiled, and from modern-day experiences of still living eye witnesses, including me, it is time to make some clear, concrete decisions.

I still remember when I first became a Jesus follower. One of the men I worked with in the aircraft industry kept bugging me. He would say things like, "You Christians use Jesus like a crutch." I would say something like, "That is true; I lean on Him all the time." He would come by my area almost every day to hurl an insult at me. One day, he came to my work area just prior to retiring. As he was adding insult to injury, I had a word for him come into my mind. After he finished his diatribe, I said the following.

"Do you know why I follow Jesus?"

He said, "You don't want to go to hell."

I said, "No, that is not the reason. I love Jesus because He has given me love, joy, peace, patience, and many other wonderful qualities. I thank Him, serve Him, and love Him because He has allowed me to have a friendship with Him here and now." In response to these statements, he said, "I know, I have seen you change as a result of being with Him."

A Decision Is Needed

I want to reiterate something I mentioned earlier, "When in the white room, seeing the hologram of the earth and the two paths, His voice speaking so lovingly, yet so authoritatively, that, 'Everyone born on earth will live forever!'" I knew that not only did I need to be very clear with God about my own decisions, but also—everyone else on earth did too. Because He allowed me that experience and burned these words into my being, the passion for everyone to choose wisely is also burning in me. This includes those who are reading this book.

The place of darkness, or the outer darkness, or hell was not made as a place for us to stay, nor even visit. It was specifically created as a place to hold the fallen angels and their self-deceived, self-appointed, egocentric leader, Satan, so that they would not be allowed to corrupt anything or anyone else—forever! (See Matthew 25:41.)

However, because God will not coerce or force anybody to serve Him, He will allow people (all of us) to make the free choice to go to heaven or hell. Had He not created us as free moral agents, if everyone just went about their lives doing everything exactly as He planned because we did not have any other options, we would be little more than robots or puppets.

Remember, sharing and returning God's love is not just a feeling, but also a conscious choice—this is where the free choice to love Him comes into play.

Some Prefer Darkness

As we've shared about Jesus with many people over the years, a realization has come to mind. Some people, either through wrong knowledge, bizarre thinking, or because they don't believe, say that they would prefer to be in the outer darkness or hell. Some have even given excuses like the following: "I won't know anybody in heaven. I'll be with my friends in hell."

They don't realize the terrible fact, that even though their "friends" may well end up there, they may never find or recognize each other and if perchance they do stumble across each other in the next million years, they would more than likely dislike each other. The reason is there is no love, affection, or friendship in hell because it is totally devoid of God ("God is love"—1 John 4:8), and every good and pleasant trait that is attributed to Him. Rather, hell is a place totally consumed by eternal hatred.

Heaven Is for Us

Heaven was not created for demons or Satan. Jesus explained that His sheep will hear the King say to them, *"Come, you who are blessed of My Father, inherit the kingdom prepared for you from the foundation of the world"* (Matthew 25:34). The heaven that I've heard of, experientially seen light from, and read about in Scripture is one of unimaginable love, light, purity, joy, and much, much more! Both descriptions of outer darkness and heaven are of real places.

If You Don't Believe Now, You Will Eventually

Someday in the not-too-distant future the heavens will roll up like a scroll and the earth that we know will be transformed and we will have a new heaven and the new earth (Revelation 21:1). And there will be a city (New Jerusalem) that will not need light generated for the supernatural light will come from God (Revelation 22:5).

There will be many heavenly beings in this new heaven and new earth. This amazing place will be filled with the things we are used to seeing here on earth, like flowers, plants, etc., but the amount of life they have and the intensity of the spectacular colors will be almost too much to comprehend—it will take our breath away to see all the amazing sights of the place.

As Paul wrote, *"But as it is written: 'Eye has not seen, nor ear heard, nor have entered into the heart of man the things which God has prepared for those who love Him'"* (1 Corinthians 2:9, NKJV). In other words, heaven is too beautiful and glorious to describe in human language. Furthermore, we will be able to do things in our new, glorified bodies which are only possible in a science fiction movie today.

A Crowd Is Waiting

First, there is God—the FATHER. We have come to know Him here, but we will know Him much better when we get into His kingdom in heaven. *"For now we see in a mirror dimly, but then face to face; now I know in part, but then I will know fully just as I also have been fully known"* (1 Corinthians 13:12).

Secondly, Jesus will also be in heaven; we will see and know Him as God—the Son. Also, we've come to know Him while here on earth, but we shall know Him in such a greater measure when we get into the fullness of the kingdom of heaven. Just from my short time seeing Him in the light and having an overwhelming wave of His love come across me, I can understand why, people who have experiences like this don't want to come back here to earth. The love that I experienced, though for such a short time, was much more than anything I've ever experienced here.

We will also know God—the Holy Spirit better. Though we have started to get to know Him here on earth, we hardly know Him at all—some only speak of Him. But when the fullness of the kingdom of God happens, the Holy Spirit will be one of our best companions and will be working with us, helping us to understand the fullness of what we've inherited. In fact, Paul called the Spirit the "earnest (down payment) of our inheritance" (Ephesians 1:14). We will no longer just have a theology of the Holy Spirit, but we will have an "experienciology" of Him; He will no longer be an abstract misty thought, but will be our closest, constant companion who is with us all the time.

There will also be heavenly beings that are different than any we have seen here in this realm. There will be an innumerable host of angels, cherubim, and seraphim, as well as other beings who may be there.

Our family, friends, and others who have passed on believing in Jesus and walking on His path for thousands of years will be waiting to greet us. Everyone who participated in writing the Bible by Holy Spirit's inspiration will be waiting to greet us. (Hint—read the Bible so you will have something to talk about when they walk up to you in heaven and ask, "How did you like my book?")

So, my friend, I would like to ask you a question. Are you ready to face the rest of your life? I'm not asking about the rest of your life here on earth. I'm asking about the rest of your eternal life, for, whether you like it or not and whether you believe it or not, you are going to live forever! Our bodies will die, but our spirit and soul will live on eternally.

Are You Ready?

You may choose to be forever in the presence of Almighty God and enjoying the most wonderful universe you can imagine; in fact, we can't even imagine it! And you'll be in the company of supernatural beings that are way beyond fictitious characters like Batman, Superman, or any other supernatural movie heroes, but, they will pale in comparison to what we will experience there!

On the Other Hand

Or, on the other hand, you have the free will to choose not to enter this most wonderful experience; forever! You can choose not to live for God; you can choose not to have a relationship with Jesus; you can choose to serve yourself, to become your own god. And, as you choose to do that there will be a rumbling, gleeful laughter echoing throughout the eons of darkness. You won't be able to hear it but there will be great anticipation for you to come and join them in their miserable glee. The other humans who are there won't be gleeful, but Satan and his cohorts will have gained another victim—perhaps thinking that they have won a little bit more of God's power. All the while, God is broken-hearted over those who have chosen not to be His friends and dwell in His kingdom. It is not His will that any should perish and be doomed in this place of darkness.

> The Lord is not slow about His promise, as some count slowness, but is patient toward you, **not wishing for any to perish** but for all to come to **repentance**" [to turn around from a life of sin and believe in Him] (2 Peter 3:9).

Why would anybody choose eternal death over life, darkness over light? Why would we continue to choose our own way instead of God's way? You may want to start reading your Bible, and if you don't have a Bible, you may want to get one so you can read it. When buying a car, there is an owner's manual that goes with the car and it lets you know how to keep the car in good shape. The manufacturer knows better than anyone else how the product should operate.

In the same way, there's an owner's manual to being human and living forever—it is called the Bible! The more of it that you and I know and understand and practice the more we will be guaranteed of a wonderful eternal blessing of a life. Also, those who have written it will be in heaven awaiting our coming.

The Choice Is Up to Us

If we end up in heaven it will be a result of our choices and the Holy Spirit Who has been drawing us to make those choices. But, inversely, if we end up in the outer darkness, we will have absolutely no one to blame but ourselves and our own stubborn choices! In researching and writing this book under the direct orders from the Holy Spirit, I have done the best I can to present the truth that has been revealed to me. I can guarantee that you will have a much more pleasant experience if you choose to figure out all your questions while you're in heaven and not in the place of darkness.

So, I urge you by the love of Christ that has rescued me from an eternal darkness and compelled me to write this book, that you choose to go to heaven with me and a myriad of others, and that you deny Satan, the enemy of your soul and of God, who will be a prisoner there forever as well. You have nothing to lose and at the same time everything to gain. If you choose light and life, a wonderful forever awaits you! If not, I don't even want to think about that! Please choose Jesus!

My hope and my prayer for you is that I will meet you in the kingdom of God on the other side of this life. We will forever enjoy His presence in the wonderful place He has created that is our chosen destiny.

The following, as promised earlier in this book, is a simple way to start your new life with God. Just read and respond to start the experience of the new birth and new path for your life. YOUR SPIRITUAL ADVENTURE IS JUST GETTING STARTED!

The following points explain how to have a personal relationship with God and experience the life for which you were created. Many years ago, a man named Bill Bright developed a simple way to seek after that relationship with God that the Bible calls being "born again." These principles are adapted from his findings. (Note: Bill Bright's The Four Spiritual Laws are reprinted in the appendix in the back of this book.)

- **God loves you!**

He wants you as one of His friends. He wants to reveal His ideal plan for you. *By this the love of God was manifested in us, that God has sent His only begotten Son into the world so that we might live through Him* (1 John 4:9).

> *"This is eternal life, that they may know You, the only true God, and Jesus Christ whom You have sent"* (John 17:3).

> *And Abraham believed God...and he was called the friend of God* (James 2:23).

Most people don't know God personally. Why? People turn away from God, either willfully or ignorantly. The things we've done which we know are wrong and those we don't know are wrong keep us from Him. The Bible calls these things "sin." Sin destroys our friendship with God. This rejected relationship is what the Bible describes as our sin. Everyone has sinned! *"For all have sinned and fall short of the glory of God"* (Romans 3:23).

If sin were a job, we would not like our wages! Someone said sin is like a credit card—you may enjoy it now, but you will pay later. *"For the wages of sin is death (eternal separation from God and in the darkness), but the free [unmerited] gift of God is eternal life in Christ Jesus our Lord"* (Romans 6:23).

God is perfect; we are sinful and we are not close to Him because of our sin. Again, the things we've done wrong are our sins. We can try to bridge this gap with being good or religious, but our sin is a barrier that keeps us separated from God. The only way to bridge this gap between people and God is through Jesus. He is the only solution for our sin. Only through Him can we become God's friends and be forgiven. Only in Him can we experience His love and plan for our lives.

- **Jesus is God!**

  He [Christ] is the image of the invisible God, the firstborn of all creation (Colossians 1:15).

- **Jesus died in our place.**

  For Christ also died for sins once for all, the just for the unjust, so that He might bring us to God" (1 Peter 3:18).

- **Jesus did not stay dead.**

  During the forty days after He suffered, died, and rose again, He appeared to the Apostles and He proved to them in many ways that He was actually alive (Acts 1:3a). His resurrection proved that He was God and that He had suffered the punishment we deserved in our place.

Jesus told him, "I am the way, and the truth and the life; No one comes to the Father but through Me" (John 14:6).

- **God proves His love.**

  "For God so loved the world, that He gave His only begotten Son, that whoever [you and me] believes in Him shall not perish, but have eternal life" (John 3:16).

We deserve separation from God forever, but, in His love, God sent Jesus to pay the penalty for our sins by dying on the cross. God has made the way for us to be forgiven, and to come close to Him and be friends. That way is Jesus. Knowing this is only a mental "starting place," each of us must place our trust in Jesus as our only Savior and Lord. Only then can we have a true friendship with Him.

We must:

- **Agree with God**—we have all sinned and must repent and turn from it (now).

- **Trust in God**—to forgive us completely based on Jesus' sacrificial death on the cross.

- **Choose to follow Jesus**—put Him first, as the #1 priority in our lives.

This friendship with Him is personal:

But as many as received Him, to them He gave the right to become children of God, even to those who believe in His name (John 1:12).

The friendship is God's gift to us:

For by grace you have been saved through faith; and that not of yourselves, it is the gift of God; not as a result of works, so that no one may boast (Ephesians 2:8-9).

He saved us, not on the basis of deeds which we have done in righteousness, but according to His mercy, by the washing of regeneration and renewing by the Holy Spirit (Titus 3:5).

To begin a friendship with God, you must place your trust in JESUS ALONE! God looks at the attitude of your heart. You can express your attitude toward God through prayer. Prayer is simply talking with God. This prayer is similar to the prayer I prayed over forty years ago. I haven't regretted it since then and I am sure you won't either. Talk to God right now and say:

Lord Jesus, I want to know you personally. I'm sorry for going my own way. Please forgive me for all my sins and things I've done wrong. Thank you for dying on the cross to pay for my sin. I agree to turn from my old ways and follow You as my Savior and Lord. Please come and take first place in my life.

Could you say this to God and mean it? Is there anything stopping you from saying this right now? I urge you to do it. Do it now!

So, How?

Did you pray the prayer in the last chapter? If so, here is a website or app that you can go use to renew and strengthen your relationship with the God you just prayed too. In iTunes look up the God Tools app by CRU and the Jesus Film Project app that allows you to see the Jesus film in over 1,000 languages.

If you are starting your walk with Him through the prayer you've just prayed, you can contact us at our website: evadingdeathsgrip.com, and let us know. We would be so blessed to hear from you. We also have materials there to help you on your spiritual path (toward the light).

Over the years of work in Singapore, upon going to a movie theater with friends and finding it "sold out," the people I was with said, "SO HOW?" This Singlish expression is translated as, "So, what to do now?" Naturally, if you have prayed the prayer offered in the last chapter, you are wondering, "SO HOW?"

The moment you received Christ by faith, as an act of the will, many things happened, including the following:

- Christ came into your life (Revelation 3:20, Colossians 1:27).

- Your sins were forgiven (Colossians 1:14).

- You became a child of God (John 1:12).

- You received eternal life (John 5:24).

- You began the great adventure for which God created you (John 10:10).

Can you think of anything more wonderful that could happen to you than receiving Christ? Would you like to thank God in prayer right now for what He has done for you? By thanking God, you demonstrate your faith.

Suggestions for Christian Growth

Spiritual growth results from trusting Jesus Christ. A life of faith will enable you to trust God increasingly with every detail of your life, and to practice the following:

G. Go to God in prayer daily (John 15:7).

R. Read God's Word daily (Acts 17:11); begin with the Gospel of John.

O. Obey God moment by moment (John 14:21).

W. Witness for Christ by your life and words (Matthew 4:19, John 15:8).

T. Trust God for every detail of your life (1 Peter 5:7).

H. Holy Spirit—allow Him to control and empower your daily life and witness

(Galatians 5:16-17, Acts 1:8, Ephesians 5:18).

Also, ask Jesus to baptize you with the power from on high so that you may be Jesus' witness, with the signs following you the Bible characterizes that follow the believer (see Mark 16:15–18, 1 Corinthians 12:1-11, Romans 12:1-8).

There are four important things you need to do once Jesus becomes Lord of your life: pray, share your story, study the Bible, and fellowship with other believers.

- **Learn to pray.**

Talk to God—that's what prayer is. Talk to God like He is your best friend and like He is right there with you, because He is. We talk to Him and He talks to us by the Holy Spirit. Pray at set times and pray spontaneously. Pray all the time—talk to Him about everything. Ask Him for His opinion on things. Attempt to follow His leading as often as possible. In other words, keep Him on the front burner of your mind.

This is what prayer involves:

o Prayer—talking openly and honestly with God.

o Praise—praising God simply for Who He is.

o Thanksgiving—thanking God for all He has already done.

o Supplication—requesting God's help in any area of need.

o Talk to Him in the morning.

o Talk to Him in the evening.

o Talk to Him all the time ("Pray without ceasing"—1 Thessalonians 5:17).

- **Tell others about your experience.**

It is very important to tell others: your friends, family members, co-workers, or anyone else you meet, about this important life change you've just had. Sharing your faith helps solidify it in your own heart and mind.

> *The word of faith which we are preaching, that if you confess with your mouth Jesus as Lord, and believe in your heart that God raised him from the dead, you will be saved; for with the heart a person believes, resulting in righteousness, and with the mouth he confesses, resulting in salvation* (Romans 10:8b-10).

- **Get a Bible.**

In order to grow spiritually, it is important that we know, understand, and live as the Word of God (the Bible) directs us. You will enjoy reading and learning how to understand the Bible. Perhaps you've tried to understand its pages prior to being "born-again."

You will find that though it has some difficult passages, God will help illuminate its words and meaning within its pages. I would recommend that you get a Bible version that is a close translation to the original Hebrew and Greek languages. The New American Standard Bible is one of the closest to the original texts of the Bible.

o **Devour the Bible.**

Like water and sunlight to a plant, a steady diet of God's Word is vital to spiritual growth. Let God cultivate within you an appetite for spiritual things. Jesus said, *"Blessed are those who hunger and thirst for righteousness, for they shall be satisfied"* (Matthew 5:6). Read the Bible as often as possible. I have been on a reading plan to read through the entire Bible every year. The first year of my experience with Jesus (over forty years ago), I read the Bible from cover-to-cover seven times. Ever since, I have read it through once a year for the past forty plus years.

When I started reading the Bible, it was because of a dream I had during my first weeks as a new follower of Christ. I dreamed that I died and went to heaven. There was a long line of people waiting to meet me there. The first man in the line came forward and shook my hand and welcomed me into heaven. His name was Habakkuk (the prophet who wrote a book named after himself in the Old Testament). I had not read it yet and I said, "Oh, no!" Then I looked down the line of all those waiting to shake my hand. Every author of the Bible was in line and excited to hear what I thought about what they had written.

I awakened almost shouting "OH, NO!" From then on, I started reading my Bible every time I got the chance.

o **Follow the teachings of the Bible.**

Read it with the thought running through your mind, "God will speak to me through these words and I will learn to apply whatever He teaches me." The principles of the Bible are of no personal benefit to us unless we apply them to our daily lives. The book of James stresses the importance of being doers of the Word, not just unchanged hearers of it (James 1:22-24).

o **Meditate on and memorize portions of Scripture.**

When I say "meditate," I do not mean like "Eastern meditation." Biblical meditation involves rehearsing spiritual truths over and over in your mind until they finally get into your spirit and become a part of your life.

You may ask yourself, "Why memorize the Bible?" Here is a good reason, *"This book of the law shall not depart from your mouth, but you shall **meditate on it day and night**, so that you may be careful to do according to all that is written in it; for then you will make your way prosperous, and then you will have success"* (Joshua 1:8-9). So, memorization and meditation on the Bible go hand-in-hand. By doing both, it can actually help you become a success in every area that it covers, which is most, if not all, situations in life.

> *How blessed is the man who does not walk in the counsel of the wicked, nor stand in the path of sinners, nor sit in the seat of scoffers! But his delight is in the law of the Lord, and in His law he meditates day and night. He will be like a tree firmly planted by streams of water, which yields its fruit in its season and its leaf does not wither; and in whatever he does, he prospers* (Psalms 1:1-3).

This is yet another promise from the Bible of prospering in whatever we do if we meditate on and apply God's Word to our everyday lives.

o **Personalize passages of Scripture.**

Here is an example from Jesus' famous words in John 3:16, *"For God so loved the world* [**me**]*, that He gave* [Jesus] *His only begotten Son, that whosoever* [that includes **me**! I am in the whosoever category] *believes in Him* [**I** do believe in Him; therefore, **I**] *will not perish, but have eternal life* [live forever in His kingdom and light]*."*

o **Study the Bible for deeper understanding.**

I recommend you use Bible Gateway on the internet at www.biblegateway.com or download some free Bible software as a helpful study tool (an excellent program can be found at www.e-sword.net). This will help you navigate and explore the Word of God as the Holy Spirit guides you into all truth. *"Your word is a lamp to my feet and a light to my path"* (Psalm 119:105). Reading the Bible is like crossing a lake in a boat just skimming across the surface; studying is like diving down underwater to explore the depths. It includes reading commentaries, Bible dictionaries, and other reference material that makes a passage come alive with rich meaning. Don't be satisfied merely skimming the surface. Determine in your mind to go deeper.

- **Fellowship with other believers.**

God's Word instructs us not to forsake *"the assembling of ourselves together"* (Hebrews 10:25). It is important to meet with other God followers. I use the words "God follower" purposefully—for they are those who attend church, who have a deep relationship with God, who are reading His Word, the Bible, and who are excited about what He is speaking to them. However, there are others who may have the outside trappings of Christianity, but who are not passionate about serving Him, reading the Bible, and loving others. So, there is a need to seek out people who will help you grow in your faith and your "experience" with God. Take your time finding them. Locate a church or group of believers that teaches the Bible and follows those teachings, whether it's a church that meets in a building or in each other's homes. My personal suggestion is an evangelistic church (one that shares the Gospel and draws people to a deep relationship with God, the Father, the Son, and Holy Spirit). Find a Spirit-filled church that reads and studies the Bible, believes in all that it says, prays for the sick, and has other "gifts" of the Spirit manifesting as well. Most of these kinds of church groups also emphasize that the "fruit of the Spirit" is as important as the gifts of the Spirit (Galatians 5:22-23). Gifts of the Holy Spirit grow from God's power manifested through us, while fruit of the Holy Spirit comes from God's love manifested through us.

If you do not belong to a local church, don't wait to be invited. Take the initiative; call the pastor of a nearby church where Christ is honored and His Word is preached. Start this week, and make plans to attend regularly. You will become rooted and grounded in your faith as you interact in a network of strong believers.

Suggested Answers

CHAPTER ONE

Fictional Movies and Eastern Spiritual Perception

1. What is the difference between the eastern understanding of "the Force" or "the Forces" (as popularized in some modern movies) and the one introduced in this book?

Answer: The force or forces in many science fiction movies is a single energy that can be manipulated for good or evil per the practice and will of the person or being manipulating it and the amount of midi-chlorians (microscopic life forms which enabled one to touch the force) within them. This force as well as the midi-chlorians is non-personal. They were "things" rather than personal beings who could be known. By manipulation of "the force" one could do small miraculous looking things, like cutting off the air to someone or sending a hypnotic suggestion for a security guard, etc. So, those who had contact with the force experienced personal power and could advance in practicing how to use it. In the real universe in which we live, there are two forces: evil and good.

Evil: resultant of a rebellion in heaven, in which Satan rebelled against God and His authority (because of pride) and one-third of the angels were persuaded or deceived to rebel with him. The rebellion's ensuing kingdom was darkness brought about through rebellion and pride.

Note: this dark kingdom has human followers who generally are of deceived minds— darkened to the understanding of the Gospel of Christ and the reality of God.

Good: which has power, love, self-control, patience, goodness, and other positive qualities of the One True God of the universes—His kingdom—one of light and love with two-thirds of the original angels. He is a personal being and desires to come into relationship and friendship with His subjects.

2. How do the two spiritual kingdoms manifest themselves on earth?

Answer: Through people mainly, though occasionally there is a "breaking through" of either kingdom into the physical realm. There is an extreme, unfathomable power associated with the kingdom of light. Jesus stated, *"All authority has been given to Me in heaven and on earth ..."* (Matthew 28:18). This power was transferred to the twelve Apostles: *"And He called the twelve together, and gave them power and authority over all the demons and to heal diseases"* (Luke 9:1). This same supernatural power has been and is being transferred to believers today by the Holy Spirit. Jesus indicated that His work would be perpetuated by His followers, *"And these signs will accompany those who have believed: in my name, they will cast out demons; they will speak with new tongues ... they will lay hands on the sick, and they will recover"* (Mark 16:17-19). This and many other subjects are being answered in the new book series we are authoring entitled, "Gifts or Gimmicks."

3. Have you ever even thought about the two spiritual kingdoms?

Answer: Most people have at some time. This thought pattern may take the form of questions like "Why do bad things happen to good people?" or "Why is there so much evil around us in this world?"

4. Do you think that there are actual spiritual beings bent on destroying us?

Answer: Yes, based on my own experience and thousands of other testimonies, I have found this to be true.

5. Is there a way to have victory over addictive behavior?

Answer: For those of us with addictive behavior patterns, we can get help and learn to curb the addictions into better ways of coping with stress, etc. One reliable program (if pursued with the whole heart) is "Celebrate Recovery," which was introduced through Saddleback Church in Lake Forest, California. The following website can direct you on how to get help. http://saddleback.com/connect/ministry/celebrate-recovery

6. Are there ways to keep ourselves from having a heart attack, even when heart disease is hereditary or is in our DNA?

Answer: Accept the things we cannot change, but change things we can (by this, it is meant that there may be certain limitations brought about by different diseases, inherited weaknesses, etc., and we may just need to realize that it won't get better barring a miracle).

Changeable things:

- Our diet—what we eat and drink has a lot to do with our health.

- Our lifestyle—sedentary versus active.

- Our sleep habits.

- Exercise, if possible.

CHAPTER TWO

The Battle, Mayday! On May Day

1. Does anything catch God by surprise?

Answer: Nothing takes God by surprise, even when He does not think about something that someone could do, He knows their "track record." And, He also knows the path of any choice a person makes.

2. Does God cause all things?

Answer: No, sometimes He allows bad things

to happen which usually result from people's poor choices. But even in bad situations, He can cause all things to work together for good to those who are called by His name and that brings glory to Him (Romans 8:28).

Some religions seem to believe that God causes all things, even evil things. A great problem this brings is that if He is responsible for all things that He causes, whenever someone is killed by someone else purposefully, this theory would place the blame on Him. This theory eliminates our responsibility for bad choices and blames God for bad things that happen. He is the author of good not evil.

Example: If someone never changes the oil in their car, when it breaks down due to the contaminated oil, their response could be: "Because God caused the car to breakdown, it must be that He did not want me to have it." So, God's will be done. Actually, the breakdown would be the result of the owner's negligence not God's interference. This does not describe the God of the Bible, in my opinion.

3. Can you give an example how something worked out for your good and God's glory?

Answer: Many situations (including my heart attack) seemingly are not to our benefit and God's glory, but as we keep trusting Him, He intervenes and turns it around for our good. Joseph told his brothers who tried to kill him and then sold him into slavery in Egypt, *"As for you, you meant evil against me, but God meant it for good in order to bring* about this present result, to preserve many people alive" (Genesis 50:20). God is a master at bringing good out of bad situations!

CHAPTER THREE
Conflicting Kingdoms, Violent Spiritual Realities

1. Do you think there are actual, personal, individual beings (demons) who are dispatched to do bad and ugly things to those of us who live here on planet earth?

Answer: Yes, the Bible and many other religious writings express this reality, as well as the experiences of many like myself who were in direct conflict with them. When revivalist Charles Finney was asked how he could believe in a devil, he responded, "Why don't you try opposing him sometime and you'll find out whether he exists or not."

2. How much power is available in the name of JESUS?

Answer: Per Matthew 28:18, Jesus said that all power and authority were His. And He transferred His power and authority first to His Apostles, then to all believers (see Mark 16:17-18, Acts 1:8, Acts 2). Note: there were initially around 120 people, not just the twelve Apostles who were "baptized in the Holy Spirit." History declares that the same Holy Spirit has done similar things since. So, how much power do we have? As much as He wants us to have and possibly up to as much as He had while here on earth. In fact, the word translated "power" in Acts 1:8, *"You will receive **power** when the Holy Spirit has come upon you,"* is from the Greek word *dunamis* from which we derive the word "dynamite." So, the Holy Spirit empowers us with the dynamic, supernatural power of God.

3. Is Jesus' power (authority) somehow transferable?

Answer: As a believer and a follower of Jesus, we have His life inside of us, therefore, His authority is living inside of us as well. *"Truly, truly, I say to you, he who believes in Me, the works that I do, he will do also; and greater works than these he will do; because I go to the Father"* (John 14:12).

> *"Go into all the world and preach the Gospel to all creation. He has believed and has been baptized shall be saved; but he who has disbelieved shall be condemned. These signs will accompany those who have believed: in My name [Jesus] they will cast out demons, they will speak with new tongues; they will pick up serpents, and if they drink of deadly poison, it will not hurt them; they will lay their hands on the sick and they will recover"* (Mark 16:15-18).

Note: believers carry some, if not all, of the authority of Jesus when they are in relationship with Him and calling on His name.

CHAPTER FOUR

Benevolent Dictator, Malevolent Foe

1. Can you point out examples of two physical or spiritual kingdoms that are diametrically opposed to each other that are on earth today?

Answer: Probably the least subtle is exemplified by the "Church of Satan" and those in the Christian churches.

Possibly, another example is the radical, militant form of Islam (terrorism) versus almost everyone else. Radical Islamists insist for all others to convert to Islam or lose their lives. Another example of the two kingdoms at war is the socialistic worldview (which is anti-God) versus the Christian-based worldview.

2. If not, why do you think otherwise?

Answer: That there are opposite kingdoms is fairly evident. But, if you don't think so, that is OK. We are not trying to convince you as much as tell the experience of Dr. Steve and others.

3. Do you believe that these kingdoms have equal power—i.e., Yin Yang (an Asian concept)?

Answer: No, it is believed that there are two kingdoms, one which is God's reign and rule and submitted loyal people, angels, etc. The other kingdom is one established by the egocentric arrogance of one renegade fallen archangel (Lucifer/Satan) and his deceived and disobedient fallen angelic beings (demons) and as many humans as they can convince to follow them.

4. Eastern religions use concepts of equal opposite forces, or in new age, etc., the "Force" that can be manipulated for either good or evil. Why are these concepts incorrect?

Answer: God cannot be "manipulated." He can be sad, pleased, and all other emotions, but we cannot coerce Him.

5. According to the Bible, what is the origin of demons?

Answer: They are angelic beings who chose to follow in Satan's rebellion against God. Most likely, if I am interpreting biblical symbolism correctly, one-third of the heavenly beings fell (Revelation 12:3-4).

6. What was the cause of Lucifer's expulsion from heaven?

Answer: His arrogance and insolent pride—he, being a "created being," stated that he would become as GOD. God is not a created being! Therefore, Satan could never achieve God-like status. Instead of being content to lead the worship of God, he coveted to be worshipped and rebellion filled his heart, resulting in his fall

7. What possibly could be in the loving purpose of God to cast Satan and one-third of the angels (the deceived, rebellious ones) to the earth?

Answer: God wants loving submission to Him

and His kingdom and a friendship with us. LOVE is not just an emotional feeling, but involves choice and decision—these two things are an act of our free will.

No War = No Victory. As God's ARMY, we must have a war in order to have victory. To be an overcomer, we must have something or someone to overcome. The devil, Satan, played right into God's hand by rebelling. Now, we have a war, but we are not the ultimate ones who will win the victory. We will battle, but in the end, God will win and we will share His victory forever and ever.

8. What kinds of love can you name? Is love just a feeling? Is it just the hormonal calling from one to another?

Answer: Love is expressed on different levels by three Greek words translated "love" in the New Testament:

- *Agape*—supernatural love, God's unconditional, self-sacrificial love flowing to us and through us to others. Paul described this love in detail in 1 Corinthians 13.

- *Philia*—brotherly love, the love shared by people with common goals and interests (i.e., Philadelphia—"The City of Brotherly Love"—or at least it started that way).

- *Eros*—from which we get the word "erotic," describes a sensual attraction or an affection of a sexual nature (Wikipedia, 2016a).

CHAPTER FIVE

Who We Are

1. Why talk about God being tripartite?

Answer: We are "created" in His image. If someone believes that men and women came from chance acting over time, it would be like taking the two and one-half million parts (approximately) of a Space Shuttle, throwing all of them into the air and expecting them to be put together and ready for launch when they came back to the ground. No matter how many times and how long you did this, it would never, ever result in a rocket. In my opinion, it takes much more faith to believe in an evolutionary start than to believe that there is one great higher being who created us!

2. What are the three parts of human beings?

Answer: The body, the soul, and the spirit.

3. What happens to the body at the point of death?

Answer: The body quits working. Its functions shut down, including heart, brain, lungs, and everything else. This is not instant in most cases, but takes a few minutes to a few hours, and depending on medical intervention, may take much longer. So, the body stops functioning and starts decaying and decomposing.

4. What happens to the soul and spirit at death?

Answer: The spirit and soul separate from the body but continue "living."

5. Where do the spirit and soul go after the body dies?

Answer: The Bible teaches that the spirit and soul continue to live, though absent from the body, eternally in either heaven or hell. There is substantial evidence that seems to indicate that a new "spiritual" body prepared for eternal life is the shell for the spirit and soul.

Note: the new body, soul, and spirit will be discussed more in the following chapters.

CHAPTER SIX

Two Paths, Two Destinations

1. Have you heard other people's stories about their spirit "floating" out of their bodies?

Answer: There are many experiences documented in many books and on many websites about these types of experiences. Even a board member spoke of being in a meeting, and, without dying, because of the intensity of the meeting, he found himself floating above and looking down at everyone there. These kinds of phenomena do happen.

2. What did you think?

Answer: I thought that it is good that he was not having a heart attack or something. But, I also realized that it is important not to say these kinds of experiences are not real. It is also quite different when the body is dead and there is no place to come back to.

3. Have you ever thought of what happens after death?

Answer: I've thought more and more about that recently.

4. What supernatural powers do you suppose we will have since there is an "afterlife"?

Answer: We don't know for sure, but it would be nice to have the supernatural abilities described in books I've researched:

- Supernatural zoom vision.
- Travel at amazing speeds.
- Floating.
- More alive than we are here on earth.
- Senses to the extreme.

5. Have you ever experienced, or heard of someone who has experienced, the presence of angels?

Answer: I've experienced their presence several times in the last forty-four years. (There is more on this subject coming in a book we are authoring currently.)

6. Have you ever experienced, or heard of someone who has experienced, the presence of demons?

Answer: Yes, I've seen them when they are in partial control of someone's life, by manifesting in evil behavior. Also, I've seen them cast out of people and leave, which is very exciting.

CHAPTER SEVEN

Destination Darkness, The End of the Other Path

1. What things have you read about that happens to people when they die?

Answer: Some state that they were in darkness and they perceived this as Hell. Others just say that it means that there is nothing after death. Still others have experienced heaven, heavenly cities, and amazing places and people.

2. Why would certain people find themselves on the path to darkness after they die?

Answer:

- They have never chosen to walk with God while on earth.

- They have refused to forgive others.

- They have rejected Christ's claims and the Gospel.

3. Are there any descriptions of the darkness that stand out in your memory?

Answer: I could literally feel the darkness coming for me and quickly removed my foot from that path and put it on the other path to the light.

4. Why is forgiveness so very important?

Answer: Since the word "forgive" was mentioned six times in "The Lord's Prayer" and its explanation, it must be vitally important that we forgive all offenses and offenders. Also, it has been proven that if we hold on to anger and other negative emotions, it can result in poor health such as ulcers, etc.

5. Why is speaking against God's Holy Spirit so dangerous?

Answer: God does not want to be likened to any false god, especially Satan, who rebelled and was booted out of heaven. Also, this is a confrontational way of stating that the Spirit whom a person sees doing good is not from God. Therefore, God is robbed of the glory and honor He is due by this kind of behavior.

6. What are the seeming consequences of doing this?

Answer: Jesus said that blasphemy against the Holy Spirit would never be forgiven. This known as "The Unpardonable Sin" (see Matthew 12:31-32). So, we must be careful not to call things God is doing a work of the devil, even if we don't understand what is happening. It is better to be safe than sorry!

7. What happens to one who rejects Christ's provision for sin?

Answer: Those who reject the sacrificial death

Jesus endured on the cross are basically saying that they prefer not to have His forgiveness. I don't fully understand this, but I would rather err on the side of accepting His love and forgiveness and do things His way than to die and realize that I rejected Him and the blessing of salvation. That would be a "forever" spiritually fatal mistake to make!

8. Please explain the statement: "the darkness was not created for humans."

Answer: God created the darkness to be a place of eternal torment and imprisonment for Satan and those angels who joined his rebellion (Matthew 25:41). Neither Satan, nor any other fallen angel, will be allowed to bother us forever. This is good news. The Book of Revelation describes the final destination of Satan, his minions, and all of those whose name are not written in the Lamb's Book of Life (see Revelation 20:10-15).

The Four Spiritual Laws

BY BILL BRIGHT

Just as there are physical laws that govern the physical universe, so are there spiritual laws that govern your relationship with God.

Law #1:
God loves you and offers a wonderful plan for your life.

- **God's Love**

  "God so loved the world that He gave His one and only Son, that whoever believes in Him shall not perish but have eternal life" (John 3:16, NIV).

- **God's Plan**

  [Christ speaking] *"I came that they might have life, and might have it abundantly"* [that it might be full and meaningful] (John 10:10).

Why is it that most people are not experiencing the abundant life? Because of Spiritual Law #2:

Law #2:

Man is sinful and separated from God. Therefore, he cannot know and experience God's love and plan for his life.

• **Man Is Sinful**

All have sinned and fall short of the glory of God (Romans 3:23).

Man was created to have fellowship with God; but, because of his own stubborn self-will, he chose to go his own independent way and fellowship with God was broken. This self-will, characterized by an attitude of active rebellion or passive indifference, is an evidence of what the Bible calls sin.

This diagram illustrates that God is holy and man is sinful. A great gulf separates the two. The arrows illustrate that man is continually trying to reach God and the abundant life through his own efforts, such as a good life, philosophy, or religion—but he inevitably fails.

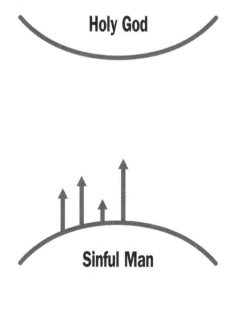

Holy God

Sinful Man

- **Man Is Separated**

  The wages of sin is death [spiritual separation from God] (Romans 6:23).

- **The third law explains the only way to bridge this gulf ...**

Law #3:

Jesus Christ is God's only provision for man's sin. Through Him you can know and experience God's love and plan for your life.

- **He Died In Our Place**

  God demonstrates His own love toward us, in that while we were yet sinners, Christ died for us (Romans 5:8).

- **He Is the Only Way to God**

  Jesus said to him, "I am the way, and the truth, and the life; no one comes to the Father but through Me" (John 14:6).

This diagram illustrates that God has bridged the gulf that separates us from Him by sending His Son, Jesus Christ, to die on the cross in our place to pay the penalty for our sins.

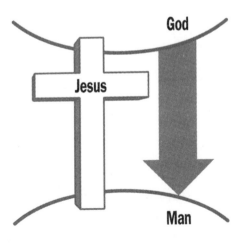

It is not enough just to know these three laws ...

Law #4:

We must individually receive Jesus Christ as Savior and Lord; then we can know and experience God's love and plan for our lives.

- **We Must Receive Christ**

  As many as received Him, to them He gave the right to become children of God, even to those who believe in His name (John 1:12).

- **We Receive Christ Through Faith**

  By grace you have been saved through faith; and that not of yourselves, it is the gift of God; not as a result of works that no one may boast (Ephesians 2:8-9).

- **When We Receive Christ, We Experience a New Birth**

  (Read John 3:1–8.)

- **We Receive Christ Through Personal Invitation**

  [Christ speaking] *"Behold, I stand at the door and knock; if any one hears My voice and opens the door, I will come in to him"* (Revelation 3:20).

Receiving Christ involves turning to God from self (repentance) and trusting Christ to come into our lives to forgive our sins and to make us what He wants us to be. Just to agree intellectually that

Jesus Christ is the Son of God and that He died on the cross for our sins is not enough. Nor is it enough to have an emotional experience. We receive Jesus Christ by faith, as an act of the will. The following explains how you can receive Christ:

These two circles represent two kinds of lives:

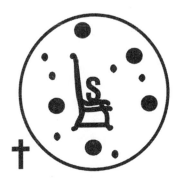 

Self-Directed Life
Christ is outside life

Christ-Directed Life
Self yielding to Christ

Which circle best represents your life?

Which circle would you like to have represent your life?

The following explains how you can receive Christ:

You Can Receive Christ Right Now by Faith Through Prayer

(Prayer is talking with God.) God knows your heart and is not so concerned with your words as He is with the attitude of your heart. The following is a suggested prayer:

Lord Jesus, I need You. Thank You for dying on the cross for my sins. I open the door of my life and receive You as my Savior and Lord. Thank You for forgiving my sins and giving me eternal life. Take control of the throne of my life. Make me the kind of person You want me to be.

Does this prayer express the desire of your heart?

If it does, I invite you to pray this prayer right now, and Christ will come into your life, as He promised.

How to Know That Christ Is in Your Life

Did you receive Christ into your life? According to His promise in Revelation 3:20, where is Christ right now in relation to you? Christ said that He would come into your life. Would He mislead you?

On what authority do you know that God has answered your prayer? (The trustworthiness of God Himself and His Word.)

The Bible Promises Eternal Life to All Who Receive Christ

God has given us eternal life, and this life is in His Son. He who has the Son has the life; he who does not have the Son of God does not have the life (1 John 5:11–12).

Thank God often that Christ is in your life and that He will never leave you (Hebrews 13:5). You can know on the basis of His promise that Christ lives in you and that you have eternal life from the very moment you invite Him in. He will not deceive you.

An important reminder …

Do Not Depend on Feelings

The promise of God's Word, the Bible—not our feelings—is our final authority. The Christian lives by faith (trust) in the trustworthiness of God Himself and His Word.

This train diagram illustrates the relationship among fact (God and His Word), faith (our trust in God and His Word), and feeling (the result of our faith and obedience). (Read John 14:21.) The train will run with or without the caboose. However, it would be useless to attempt to pull the train by the caboose. In the same way, as Christians we do not depend on feelings or emotions, but we place our faith (trust) in the trustworthiness of God and the promises of His Word.

End Notes

1. "Bipartite (Theology)," Wikipedia, https://en.wikipedia.org/wiki/Bipartite (theology). (Accessed April 12, 2017).

2. Hendrik Lorenz, "Ancient Theories of Soul," Stanford Encyclopedia of Philosophy (Summer 2009 Edition). Edward N. Zalta (ed.), (2009) https://plato.stanford.edu/archives/sum2009/entries/ancient-soul. (Accessed April 12, 2017).

3. John Burke, "Imagine Heaven," Ibook: Baker Publishing Group. Baker Books, 2015. I-book. https://itunes.apple.com/us/book/imagine-heaven/id1046985310?mt=11. p. 372.

4. Ibid., p. 52.

5. Ibid., p. 50.

6. Howard Storm, "My Descent Into Death," iBooks. https://itun.es/us/jSDdz.l pp. 9-28.

7. Ibid., pp. 30-31.

8. Ibid., pp. 9-32.

9. Storm, "My Descent Into Death," p. 39.

10. Ibid., p. 40.

11. Ibid., pp. 41-42.

12. Ibid., pp. 43-44.

13. Kevin Williams, "People Have Near-Death Experiences While Brain Dead," Near-Death Experiences and the Afterlife, http://www.near-death.com/science/evidence/people-have-ndes-while-brain-dead.html#a02. (Accessed April 12, 2017).

14. Burke, "Imagine Heaven," pp. 35-42.

15. Dr. Kenneth Ring, "Scientific Evidence Supporting Near-Death Experiences and the Afterlife," Journal of Near-Death Studies (1993). Published electronically 2016. http://www.near-death.com/science/evidence.html#a8. (Accessed April 12, 2017).

16. Every Student, "What Is Heaven Like? Is There really a Heaven?" EveryStudent.com A Safe Place to Explore Questions About Life and God (2017). Published electronically 2016. http://www.everystudent.com/forum/heaven2.html.

17. "New Jerusalem" and "Heaven," en.wikipedia.org/wiki/New Jerusalem. (Accessed April 12, 2017).

Bibliography

Burke, John. *Imagine Heaven*. *Ibook:* Baker Publishing Group, Grand Rapids, MI. 2015

Gateway.com, Bible. *637 Bible results for "Heaven."* https://www.biblegateway.com/quicksearch/?qs_version=NASB&quicksearch=heaven&startnumber=26. 2017.

Lorenz, Hendrik. *Ancient Theories of Soul*. Stanford Encyclopedia of Philosophy (Summer 2009 Edition), Edward N. Zalta (ed.) https://plato.stanford.edu/archives/sum2009/entries/ancient-soul. 2009.

Ring, Dr. Kenneth. *Scientific Evidence Supporting Near-Death Experiences and the Afterlife*. Journal of Near-Death Studies. http://www.near-death.com/science/evidence.html - a8. 1993.

Stedman, Ray. *Born of the Spirit.* www.raystedman.org/new-testament/john/born-of-the-spirit. 1983.

Student, Every. *What Is Heaven Like? Is There Really a Heaven?* EveryStudent.com. A SafePlace to Explore Questions About Life and God. http://www.everystudent.com/forum/heaven2.html. 2017.

Wikipedia. *Agape*. https://en.wikipedia.org/wiki/Agape. 2016.

Wikipedia. *Bipartite* (theology). https://en.wikipedia.org/wiki/Bipartite_(theology) 2016.

Wikipedia. *Hell*. Retrieved from https://en.wikipedia.org/wiki/Hell. 2016.

Wikipedia. *New Jerusalem:* Description. https://en.wikipedia.org/wiki/New_Jerusalem. 2016.

Williams, Kevin. *People Have Near-Death Experiences While Brain Dead.* http://www.near-death.com/science/evidence/people-have-ndes-while-brain-dead.html - a02. 2016.

ABOUT THE AUTHOR

Steven W. Long, Ed.D. serves as the assistant professor of leadership and financial freedom, via distance learning in two Taiwan universities. Dr. Long is the Co-Founding International Director of *Global Champions*, an education NPO, teaching life skills, problem solving, and character development for all levels of schools and leaders.

He has publications in several disciplines, including:

- *Freedom Through Forgiveness,* Anaheim, California

- *Freedom From the Past,* Anaheim, California

- *Short Term Effects of the Champions Project.* ProQuest (Dissertation)

- *The Word of Knowledge: A Historical, Biblical, and Applicational Study*

After experiencing a heart attack and subsequent NDEs while in Taiwan, this book attempts to discuss those experiences, as well as other spiritual issues. Dr. Long has personally researched around 1,500 sources of NDEs and out-of-body experiences, and has become an experiential and well-read expert in the field of NDEs.